MARCUS ZEPF (ED.)

Greenery in the City
Innovative and Sustainable Planning with Urban Flora

T0337640

jovis

The publication is the result of the research project "Greenery in the City" carried out by the Institut d'urbanisme de Grenoble (IUG) and financed by ELCA.

Cover: Region Stuttgart, Shutterstock

Translation into English: Lynne Kolar-Thompson
English copy-editing: Mara Taylor
Design: Institut d'urbanisme de Grenoble (IUG)
Setting: jovis Verlag: Yvonne Illig
Lithography: Bild1Druck, Berlin
Printing and binding: Graspo CZ, a. s., Zlín

Bibliographic information published by the Deutsche Nationalbibliothek
The Deutsche Nationalbibliothek lists this publication in the Deutsche Nationalbibliografie; detailed bibliographic data are available on the Internet at http://dnb.d-nb.de

jovis Verlag GmbH
Kurfürstenstraße 15/16
10785 Berlin

www.jovis.de

jovis books are available worldwide in selected bookstores. Please contact your nearest bookseller or visit www.jovis.de for information concerning your local distribution.

ISBN 978-3-86859-362-4

Greenery
in the City

A Strategy for more Greenery in Cities

Emmanuel Mony, President of the ELCA

European politics need to focus more on the topic of greenery and nature. We should educate our citizens and decision-makers even more about the economic and social values of urban greenery—from historical, botanical, and private gardens to parks and roadside greenery.

The ELCA drives the "Green City" initiative, a program jointly founded by German and Dutch organizations with the objective of preserving and developing urban public greenery. In addition to its work in Germany and the Netherlands, the "Green City" project is also currently being successfully implemented in Switzerland, France, Spain, and Ireland.

The ELCA believes in the universal importance of this topic because the fundamental questions surrounding it are the virtually same in all cities: what positive city-planning, social, and ecological effects can greenery generate? How can one best finance and maintain green areas within cities? Which plants and vegetation systems are the most beneficial? What positive effects do plants and especially trees have in reducing fine-particle pollution?

Significantly, greenery has a far greater economic and social value than generally assumed. You can find further German-language information about "Green City" activities online at www.die-gruene-stadt.de.

The ELCA strives to further an optimal relationship between transport, culture, tourism, economy, and urban greenery. After all, only the right greenery in the right place can have a positive and long-term effect. Therefore, we are always on the lookout for new projects to which we can contribute our expertise, cooperation, and support. We wish you luck and success with realizing your related goals!

The European Landscape Contractors Association, ELCA, represents sixteen national trade associations in Europe. Around 50,000 companies in the fields of gardening, landscaping, and sports-field construction provide employment for 330,000 people throughout Europe. The main tasks of these medium-sized enterprises are creating and maintaining household gardens, rooftop greenery, residential outdoor spaces, public parks, sports fields, and all kinds of green areas.

Greenery in the City
City by the Water

Without a doubt, nature is an important aspect of the contemporary city. Urban green areas satisfy manifold social needs; the growing demand for them points to an increasing ecological awareness in urban societies. This book aims to show important trends in current planning practices. Using innovative European case studies from five countries, it demonstrates how natural spaces are designed, upgraded, and integrated within cities. Furthermore, all selected regions and greenery projects involve waterways, which in itself reflects current changes in the relationship between the city and its environment. Finally, in each national context, the projects highlight two separate geographical levels—that of the municipal area and that of the district—which reveal specific and interconnected dynamics. This multilevel approach provides a more complete understanding of nature's complex role within the urban context.

On a municipal level, the following projects are presented:
> the Stuttgart Region Landscape Park (Germany)
> the "Green Fingers" concept in the city of Helsinki (Finland)
> integrated water management in the city of Breda (Netherlands)
> the Parc de la Deûle Park in the south of the municipalities association Lille Métropole (France)
> the planned Green Grid in East London (United Kingdom)

These exemplary cases help analyze important urban planning questions. For example, to what extent—in the face of increasing urban sprawl—can nature serve as a basis for territorial cohesion, as an "infrastructure" for a network of smooth mobility and habitat connectivity, or as the substrate of a "Slow City"?

On a district level, the following projects were selected:
> the water gardens in Lyon by La Confluence (France)

> the consideration of nature in the densely inhabited, artificial islands Borneo & Sporenburg in Amsterdam (Netherlands)
> the Katariina Beach Park on a former oil port site in the town of Kotka (Finland)
> the approach to the environment and to the landscape within natural areas as part of the revitalization of the former industrial district on the banks of the Karl Heine Canal in Leipzig (Germany)
> the Greenwich Millennium Village (United Kingdom)

The selected cases demonstrate innovative socio-spatial developments and planning trends that highlight the importance of spatial interactions between local and regional green areas. Small areas of greenery within the broader urban context, such as roadside greenery and residual spaces, provide a potential network for an overarching ecological concept. Urban greenery, combined with suburban agricultural and recreational spaces, helps to redefine boundaries between city and countryside. Greenery in the city can also further social relationships between younger and older generations, and it can foster a sense of responsibility for one's environs.

Furthermore, nature has a continuous and ever-changing effect on the cityscape. This fact represents a potential for transformation, something that many spatial planners and policy-makers have already recognized and harnessed. Those projects and plans that follow a green-city logic also encourage people to view degraded geographical environments with new eyes and to contextualize them more broadly. In general, a city's broader context has gained even more importance recently with the increasing competition between cities and regions.

This book therefore seeks to address the symbolic power of urban nature without neglecting the concrete aspects—including the economic dimension—of the intersections between city and nature.

Germany
Finland
France
Netherlands
United
Kingdom

Stuttgart Region
Landscape Park

H. KIRCHHOFF & M. SCHULTE

The Project's Innovative Aspects

The Stuttgart Region Landscape Park consists of the Neckar, Rems, Limes, and Albtrauf Landscape Parks. It was set up to safeguard the living environment for people, flora, and fauna, as well as support business in Stuttgart. The Stuttgart region is one of the densest agglomerations in Germany. Therefore, it is important to consider the development not only of housing, infrastructure, and transport, but also of outdoor and recreational areas, as these soft locational factors contribute significantly to a region's appeal. The park does not restrict the use of the landscape, but instead promotes its diversity and its use for agriculture and forestry, while interacting positively with the area's housing, business, and technical infrastructures.

In 1994, in response to a law supporting regional cooperation, the local government founded the Stuttgart Regional Association (Verband Region Stuttgart) to serve as the region's political voice. Every five years, citizens elect its members. In 2005, the association began sponsoring the regional landscape park, providing a conceptual framework for the master plans and enabling the association to co-finance the individual landscape park projects. They are using a two-pronged approach: firstly, according to a bottom-up (or grassroots) principle, the subspace concepts are developed in cooperation with the local authorities, expert authorities, and other involved parties. The second part consists of co-financing the projects selected by the Stuttgart Regional Association. The concept of the Stuttgart Region Landscape Park depends on the financial situation of the local authorities, as well as on political willingness.

The guiding principle of the Stuttgart Region Landscape Park is "not only to protect the landscape, but also to upgrade and shape it." This means that the landscape must also be made usable for local recreation and tourism, for example, by creating cycle paths. The individual Neckar, Rems, Limes, and Albtrauf park sections are interconnected as the Stuttgart Region Landscape Park.

Involved Parties

The Stuttgart Regional Association, local authorities, organizations, and citizens all play a role in making the Stuttgart Region Landscape Park. The bottom-up design approach guarantees that all involved parties contribute their input and cooperate with each other. Without this cooperation, the project could not be realized.

The process of drawing up individual master plans demonstrates how well this cooperation works. The local authorities and other involved parties develop ideas and projects in workshops, which then flow into master plans and landscape analyses that detail the specific characteristics, strengths, and weaknesses of the respective regions. Because they are implemented over a long period of time, the individual master plans can be modified as requirements change. The master plan also establishes overall guiding principles for each landscape park.

The regional landscape park functions as an informal tool in a competition between various regions. This informality means that its use is not limited by laws and, therefore, is flexible and can evolve freely. The landscape park should supplement existing formal tools for securing and protecting outdoor spaces by transforming the landscape through methods of active design, formation, and valorization. Overall, this will contribute to developing a "green infrastructure" that is set against the development of a "gray infrastructure."

Financial Framework

The Stuttgart Regional Association finances an apportioned share of the projects included in the master plans. Participating regional authorities also contribute to the project's financing, depending on their region's taxable capacity and population. The maximum contribution is 50%. Competitions, to which local authorities submit ideas, determine the co-financing of various projects. An idea is judged on its quality and compliance with the regional landscape park's guiding principles. A jury of regional politicians selects the winning projects. The competition's informal procedure is flexible and non-bureaucratic. The jury has a free hand in deciding which projects to award. Furthermore, local authorities without a master plan can also participate. Overall, local authorities have reacted positively to this procedure.

After a project's implementation, the Stuttgart Regional Association carries no responsibility for further maintenance and upkeep. Thus, the project demands no further resources nor additional investments from the association. Consequently,

under the co-financing arrangement, the local authorities commit themselves to maintaining the project for at least fifteen years in order to ensure the region's long-term improvement.

In addition to co-financing, further funding is provided by the INTERREG program, which can generate external resources and realize partial projects.

Overall, this has only a minimal impact on the local economy. As a rule, the funded projects are small projects, which therefore also bring about only small improvements.

Special Features

The Stuttgart Region Landscape Park displays certain special features. Firstly, the contribution of various parties to the master plans has not been a common approach up until now. It ensures that the opinions of all involved and of the local communities are represented. The inclusion of multiple parties supports a common identity within the Stuttgart region and further motivates the local authorities to maintain the result even after the projects' realization. The aim is to achieve long-term improvement to the region.

By using a free competition instead of a traditional funding concept, the Stuttgart Regional Association is free to make decisions and can react flexibly to changes.

The Stuttgart Region Landscape Park will contribute to creating a "green infrastructure" in the dense Stuttgart region, forming a counterpoint to the "gray infrastructure" and making the region attractive for residents and tourists.

Leipzig
District by the Weiße Elster and the Karl Heine Canal

H. KIRCHHOFF & M. SCHULTE

The Project's Innovative Aspects

German reunification in 1990 heralded changes for Leipzig. In 2000, the Urban Development Plan for Housing and Urban Renewal (STEP W + S) laid important foundations for developing the inner-city residential neighborhoods. Following this, the Conceptual Urban District Plan Leipzig West (KSP West) was agreed upon in 2005, proposing far-reaching measures for the Gründerzeit district of Plagwitz. New objectives and guidelines were established that will enhance Plagwitz's appeal and the quality of life there; they outline strategic and long-term urban development through 2020.

This strategy centers on building distinctive structures in Plagwitz that shape the district's cityscape, such as monuments, bodies of water, and railroad embankments. The neighborhood's development therefore focuses on specific areas. In the context of city greenery, upgrading measures for public space include installing waterside greenery, developing green zones on former railroad embankments, and continually upgrading the street areas. There is a special focus on "creating and interlinking green areas" (Leipzig 2005, p. 16).

Parallel to the Auenwald forest in the east, a further green strip (GleisGrünZug) that runs north-south will be created in the west on the former site of the Plagwitz freight train station. Strips of open space running east-west link the two large green areas, such as the Plagwitz District Park, an area for leisure and recreation that was created as part of the EXPO 2000 World Exposition on a former loading station site by the Karl Heine Canal.

The Karl Heine Canal and the Weiße Elster River form structuring elements within the Plagwitz District. Large investment sums were made available for upgrading and extending the Karl Heine Canal towards the Lindenau Harbor. In recent years, the embankment areas have been restructured, and the historic bridge connections have been repaired. In conjunction with this, a cycle path network was installed along the canal. New, little canal crossings increase the appeal of the already existing water landscape, and improve the recreational options available to Plagwitz District residents. The planned network of waterways will create a new local recreational area in the heart of the city.

The possibility, which is currently under development, of a direct boat connection—from Lindenau Harbor via the Karl Heine Canal into the city center and to the Leipzig Lake landscape to the south—will further interlink and improve the greenery and waterway systems in the city of Leipzig (City of Leipzig 2006). The planned extension of the Karl Heine Canal towards the Lindenau Harbor will provide additional development opportunities in the Plagwitz District.

The European Regional Development Fund (ERDF 2007–2013) provided initial funding for the KSP West Project, and further funding was granted in 2009.

Involved Parties

The main responsibility for drawing up the district plan and for further developing the neighborhood lies with a municipal administration project group, which is advised by external experts. Furthermore, the Forum Leipzig Westen (Forum for Leipzig West) provides a platform for involved parties to share mutual interests. On the forum, businesses, citizens, and associations can put forward their ideas and shape the area's further development together. Also, the Neighborhood Gardens Association provides a special platform for developing inner-city green areas, advocating urban gardening as a way to facilitate the intermediary use of former wastelands (Forum Leipziger Westen).

An urban development plan includes a model for future development, a transformation plan—which proposes potential restructuring in the city through 2020—and an action field plan, which suggests concrete measures to implement. Contrary to urban development framework plans, detailed and plot-specific guidelines are consciously avoided.

Financial Framework

Owing to the increasingly tight budget situation in the Municipality of Leipzig, a combination of various funding bodies was consciously chosen. First of all, traditional urban development funding schemes made significant funding contributions—in particular, Urban Regeneration in Redevelopment Areas and Urban Reconstruction East. At the moment, under the purview of these schemes, there are six redevelopment areas with various focuses in the west of Leipzig. Restructuring the Karl Heine Canal and creating a pedestrian and cycle path alongside it cost about 5.5 million euros. Further public investments were allocated to rebuilding and repairing the brick arched bridges crossing the canal (7.8 million euros) and repurposing former rail track areas for pedestrian and cycle paths (Green Fingers: 1.1 million euros).

Secondly, the EU funding scheme URBAN II, is particularly important for development in the west of Leipzig. From 2001–2008, a subsidy of around 14.5 million euros was made available. The focus was on quality improvement in the urban environment, as well as on developing the local economy and strengthening social qualities (Leipzig 2005, p. 43 et seq.). Since 2009, the Plagwitz District has been supported by the ERDF 2007–2013 funding scheme. The funding is mainly directed towards long-term and sustainable urban development and the revitalization of abandoned areas, such as transforming Lindenau Harbor into an "attractive city district" by the water.

The municipally projects have prompted private investors to get involved; their projects contribute to an improved quality of life in the neighborhood between Karl Heine Canal and the Weiße Elster. The positive effects can already be seen in the increasing number of residents and tertiary services and in the cultural activity, which is evident in the arrival of galleries, artists, and innovative companies.

Special Features

Like other East German cities after Germany's reunification, post-socialist urban transformation processes mark the city, especially its western portion. In Leipzig Plagwitz, this process took the form of transforming a former industrial and working-class quarter into a waterside city district with an exceptional quality of life. Building on the soft location factors of the Karl Heine Canal and the Weiße Elster, it was possible to realize sustainable urban development. However, the process of regenera-

tion is not yet complete. The City of Leipzig continues to pursue its urban environmental improvement strategy through the targeted development of waterway structures. Coupled with the focused development of green and open spaces in areas formerly occupied by rail tracks and other industrial sites, this has upgraded public space. In a targeted manner, abandoned and empty areas are being further developed, in order to counteract trading-down effects within the quarter. As part of this plan, the City has installed various green networks of paths and district parks lining the redeveloped waterways.

Following from the restructuring and regeneration processes, the recreational and cultural facilities, in particular, have been continuously improved in recent years. Restaurants, a canoe and rowing boat rental service, and the youth center "Kanal 28" have sprung up along the Karl Heine Canal and the Weiße Elster. The passenger ship MS Weltfrieden further promotes the canal's tourist uses, as does the annual water festival. Owing to the new and restructured pedestrian and cycle paths, the Karl Heine Canal can now be appreciated as a recreational area.

The neighborhood by the Karl Heine Canal and the Weiße Elster has now become one of Leipzig's most sought-after residential and business areas. This high level of private investment in residential housing—as well as the ensuing reduction in property and site vacancies—proves the area's long-term viability. Rising numbers of residents and the increasing demand for recreational facilities also indicate the anticipated success.

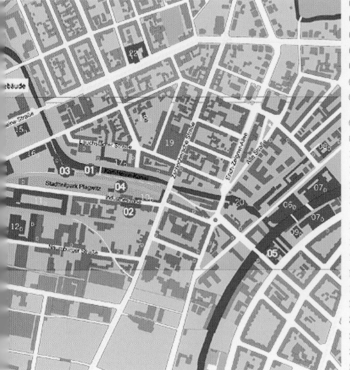

01_Stabbogenbrücke

02_Stadthäuser Industriestraße

03_Stelzenhaus[D]

04_Stadtteilpark Plagwitz mit altem Verladebahnhof[D]

05_Stadthäuser >> Sweetwater >> Holbeinstraße

06_Buntgarnwerke & Loftwohnungen >> Elsterlofts[D]

07_Buntgarnwerke // Handel, Dienstleistung, Büros, Gewerbe, Loftwohnungen[D]

08_Museum für Druckkunst[D]

09_ehemaliges Heizhaus[D]

10_Stadthausprojekt >> Wagnersche Häuser[D]

11_Konsumzentrale[D] Architekt: Fritz Höger

12_Städtischer Gewerbehof[D]

13_Technologie- und Gewerbepark Plagwitz // Business-Innovation-Center

14_Parkhaus

15_GaraGe // Jugendtechnologiezentrum[D]

16_Gewerbezentrum Weißenfelser Straße[D]

17_Feuerwache[D]

18_Mütterzentrum[D]

19_Einkaufszentrum >> Elsterpassage

20_Studiogebäude >> MDR Riverboat

21_Baumwollspinnerei[D]

22_Schaubühne Lindenfels[D]

23_Kanal 28[D]

Germany
Finland
France
Netherlands
United
Kingdom

Helsinki
Master Plan 2002, Greater Helsinki Vision 2050 & Green Fingers

MATHIEU PERRIN

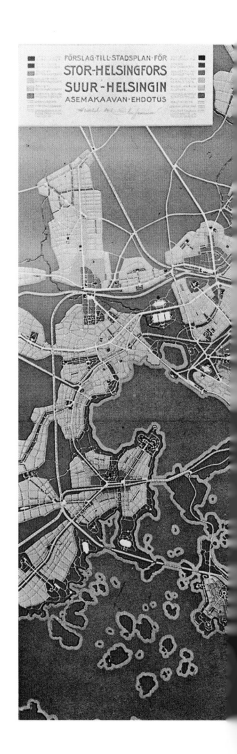

The Project's Innovative Aspects

In 2002, there were 5654 hectares of public green space within the 187-square-kilometer urban area. This represents 4.2 hectares of green space per 1,000 inhabitants. Of the green areas, 63% is municipal forest, 17% is park landscape, and 11% is fields and meadows. As part of the Master Plan 2002, which was issued in 2003 and came into effect in 2006, the municipal authorities of Helsinki proposed a network of green spaces. Natural areas, parks, and green belts will be combined so that the various green areas are interlinked, making it possible to walk from one to the other. The ensemble is arranged around major natural axes and the so-called Green Fingers, which traverse the city from the coast and stretch into the inland area (see Master Plan 2002 and its network structure of Green Fingers). The City of Helsinki's municipal planning authorities established the boundaries and positions of the landscaped areas on the basis of functional, visual, and ecological criteria. In particular, they reconnected these areas to central elements in the natural geographical framework—the rivers and coasts.

In 2006, the Finnish Ministry of the Environment and fourteen towns and boroughs in the Helsinki region oversaw the international competition Greater Helsinki Vision 2050. The purpose was to gather strategic, innovative ideas and trends for a metropolitan area that covers an area of circa 3,000 square kilometers. At the end of 2007, the jury—consisting of politicians, local experts, and university professors—selected proposals deemed appropriate for Helsinki's future development. Even if the natural dimension was not necessarily the central topic of the competition, it proved an important criterion for the evaluation process.

Project Emerald, submitted by the agency WSP Finland and the architect Juha Eskolin, emerged as the winner of this competition. The architects persuaded the jury with their forward-thinking consideration of natural spaces within Helsinki's urban region. The concept proposes a network of natural spaces manifesting

around the Green Fingers between the coast and inland. In the area around the natural axes, the same pattern continues on quite a different scale, forming a new overall structure that can be perceived on a municipal scale.

The Function and Role of Greenery in the City

In Helsinki's urban region, the natural areas primarily serve as recreation. Even before ecological concerns raised public awareness around the notion of "green consciousness" in the nineteen-seventies, the local population had already been using these spaces intensively for recreational activities; thus, people have a long-standing affinity with these natural spaces. Furthermore, through the Green Fingers' pattern, which forms part of the urban fabric, the municipal authorities have provided many inhabitants access to the city's natural areas. Promenades and paths serve to make the Green Fingers accessible to all inhabitants in less than a fifteen-minute walk. Furthermore, the closely knit web woven around the Green Fingers promotes soft mobility, meaning car-free infrastructures.

The analyses considered in the Master Plan 2002 paid close attention to natural and cultural heritage. They argued that the city and its inhabitants benefit greatly if the city's administration protects its areas of ecological interest as well as its public gardens and nineteenth-century parks.

In order to counteract urban sprawl on a regional level, the authors of Project Emerald planned to upgrade the built-up areas and to frame them with a green belt. According to those who developed the concept, an increase in agriculture near the city— closer to the consumer—is also a means of guaranteeing high-quality green areas. In this respect, the proposal for the metropolitan area proposed in the "Greater Helsinki Vision 2050" competition differs from the guidelines of the Master Plan 2002, as the latter document does not prioritize agriculture. This contrast can probably be explained by the competition's larger scale and its long-term horizon. The most important point is the proposal of the green structure as a strategic planning element on a local and geopolitical level for the Helsinki urban region. The natural areas form the connecting element for a common vision. With the help of the parties involved within the metropolitan region, this enabled many difficulties that had previously stood in the way of such a project to finally be overcome. The idea of a green structure, even if coincidental, has left lasting traces in Helsinki's planning history. In 1918, the architects Eliel Saarinen,

Einar Sjöström, and Bertel Jung—the latter was employed at the time as a municipal planner— published an initial plan for extending a nearby area, which later was developed as part of the city of Helsinki (Pro Helsingfors). This planning document, which was financed by private means, was new for the era and proposed incorporating the parks and the agricultural areas that had spatially separated the city's built-up zones from each other. Although the initial plan was never realized, many of the ideas put forward later influenced local spatial organization (see plan Pro Helsingfors). After the nineteen-seventies, planning documents covering the entire municipal region (not including the lake areas) were authorized for the first time. Subsequently, a green, radial structure was gradually developed, stretching from the coast though the city into the inland area—the "Green Fingers" consisting of parks, forests, meadows, and fields.

The Master Plan 2002 did not break with what was already there, but, on the contrary sought to integrate the historic dimension and the spatial reality. Significantly, Project Emerald also relies heavily on historical spatial concepts in a forward-looking manner.

Involved Parties

The following parties were involved in drawing up and implementing the operations of the Master Plan 2002:

- The City of Helsinki (which owns around 70% of the municipal area; selected municipal delegates voted on components of the Master Plan)
- The Planning Department of the City of Helsinki (consideration and drawing up of the plans)
- The Department of Public Construction Works with its various departments (planning, construction, renovation, maintenance of green areas)
- The Department for the Environment of the City of Helsinki (protection and maintenance of natural areas)
- Private companies appointed by the Department of Public Construction Works (realization and maintenance of the projects)
- The inhabitants of Helsinki participating in the Master Plan program (voluntary participation and support that contributes to preserving the green areas of the city.)

The following parties are involved in the international competition Greater Helsinki Vision 2050:

- Fourteen cities and municipalities of the Helsinki agglomeration (Helsinki, Espoo, Vantaa, Kauni-

ainen, Kerava, Tuusula, Järvenpää, Nurmijärvi, Mäntsälä, Pornainen, Hyvinkää, Kirkkonummi, Vihti, and Sipoo), as well as the Finnish Ministry of the Environment, which is responsible for launching and the financing the competition
- The jury, composed of representatives from the political and science spheres, as well as other experts
- Eighty-six competition participants, including the winning team Project Emerald: the firm WSP Finland with the architects Juha Eskolin, Jenni Lautso, Ilona Mansikka, and Tuomas Vuorinen

Apart from the Master Plan 2002, the City of Helsinki also gave the go-ahead for the Green Area Program for the period of 1999-2008. This program's main content is a plan in which municipalities designate areas that protect and preserve green and open spaces. The Master Plan 2002 takes account of the guidelines established in the document.

The City of Helsinki distinguishes itself in particular through its tendency to invite international bids for urban development and open space planning competitions. In 2011, for example, it initiated a competition for development strategies for the Eteläsatama area near the city center. In 2012, tenders were invited for a competition for a modern lighting concept for the city district Kruunuvuorenranta.

Financial Framework

The Helsinki City Council decides every year how much funding will be allocated for creating and maintaining green areas within the city, whereby certain projects are prioritized according to recommendations by the Department for Road Construction and Green Spaces at the Office of Public Works. The office assesses the maintenance requirements of the various green and open spaces. In 2005, it initiated the program "Good Things

The green structures and natural spaces (Green Fingers) set out in the Master Plan 2002 are not necessarily for creating new park areas, but more for linking the various existing structures in order to generate new landscape formations. It is especially important to raise awareness of the city's diverse urban greenery. The Master Plan does not contain any revolutionary concepts, but instead serves as an orientation framework that helps strengthen and preserve existing green structures.

The idea of holistically considering the network of natural spaces (Green Fingers) on the metropolitan level of all Helsinki presents great challenges.

Therefore new strategies have to be devised for bringing the many involved parties together. However, natural spaces also have to be seen in the regional context, and for the agglomeration of Helsinki it appears to make sense to set this goal on an institutional level. Contrary to the transport infrastructure, planners do not necessarily view investments in public green spaces as beneficial. Using natural spaces as a structuring spatial element for the metropolis's cityscape counts as an innovative approach, which contributes to understanding city and nature as a networked system.

Planning outdoor spaces serves a role larger than just organizing the space itself. As an important structuring element based on institutional and political decisions, the planning of outdoor spaces has the capacity to create and strengthen cohesion between Helsinki's individual communities. It does so by linking existing green areas and creating new park landscapes. Competitions for urban development and outdoor space planning serve as an important tool for generating new ideas and concepts. The City of Helsinki has taken this approach for a number of years, and it has resulted in significant successes.

Grown in Helsinki," which sought to motivate the inhabitants of Helsinki to participate voluntarily in tending public green spaces. Through the support of private companies, additional funding was secured for the purposes of planning public space.

Kotka
Katariina Beach Park

MATHIEU PERRIN

The Project's Innovative Aspects

The Katariina Beach Park stretches over twenty hectares at the southern tip of Kotka's central island. The layout of this natural space as a park for people to enjoy the area's ecology represents a turning point in the history of the city of Kotka. Interestingly, the park originally served an industrial function. In the nineteen-thirties and forties, several storage tanks for hydrocarbons were installed in this area in conjunction with the rise of Kotka's oil port. In the fifties and sixties, when the complex was most active, the industrial site was extended. It totaled up to fifty-six storage tanks and had a storage capacity of 400,000 cubic meters. In 2000, when the port industry relocated to a nearby area and the lease agreements with the oil companies expired, the city was able to consider re-purposing the site.

The on-site companies were contractually obliged to clean up the site. Between 2003 and 2006, they sanitized 100,000 tons of earth that had been contaminated by hydrocarbons, solvents, or lead. In the autumn of 2004, the Kotka municipal authorities put forward their initial proposals for creating a park. Building work started immediately, following this outline, and ran parallel to the sanitation measures. Since autumn 2006, the park has been accessible to the public, but work is still ongoing. There are plans to extend the park.

In 2012, the Katariina Beach Park received two important awards. The European Landscape Contractors Association awarded it the international trend prize Building with Greenery. Among other things, the jury highlighted the exemplary character of this transformation of a polluted industrial wasteland into a public and green recreational area. Furthermore, the Central Association of Finnish Landscaping (Puutarhaliitto ry) and the Confederation of Finnish Construction Industries (Rakennusteollisuus RT ry) awarded it the 2012 Eco-design Prize. Every year the committee awards one project on the basis of its outstanding aesthetic, functional, and environmentally friendly qualities. The committee recognized that the park has high recreational value.

In particular, this park excels at providing visitors a diversity of uses. Some spaces and facilities are dedicated mainly to sports and leisure activities (a generous lawn area, a beach volleyball court, a skate park, disc golf baskets, children's playgrounds, and outdoor fitness equipment), while others serve social purposes (picnic and barbecue areas) or are intended for walking and meditation (pedestrian paths through areas rich in flora and fauna, viewing points and seating, a meditation labyrinth, an isolated islet featuring symbolic anchor). The park is conceived as a place for encounters for all generations. The greenery, which combines planted areas, stone forms, and bodies of water, also creates a new relationship to the environment. The park developers' efforts to promote biodiverse living environments on this formerly polluted area mark its transition from an industrial to a greener phase. The park offers its visitors the opportunity to rediscover this area. Among other things, an observation tower was installed for watching birds that nest in the neighboring alder forest or in the park's wetlands.

The greenery also has a positive influence on the city's image. It has brought about a new perception of this area covering the southern tip of Kotka's central island, which had previously been associated with the local oil port industry. This positive effect spreads to the whole agglomeration, which has at times suffered as a result of its loss of economic importance. As a symbol of this development, it was recently decided to restore the ruins of Katariina Fort, an eighteenth-century structure that had been wedged between storage tanks for hydrocarbons since the nineteen-fifties.

The decline of the oil port and its industry during the final decades of the twentieth century posed a considerable problem for several Finnish waterside cities. Although the relocation of these activities to areas farther from the city in some cases freed up these sites for other interesting uses, the negative image of the former industrial area still persisted, often affecting the whole city. Changing this image was therefore a challenge. In order to do so, several cities—such as Helsinki-Jätkäsaari, Helsinki-Kalasatama, or Oulu-Toppilansaari—launched com-

prehensive development projects on the former port sites.

In the mid-eighties, the idea started to emerge in Kotka of transforming this former industrial and port city into a cluster of parks and gardens with the hope that nature would renew the city's image and local identity. Since then, the municipal authorities have introduced an incremental procedure supplementing Kotka's green network step by step, with new projects that complement its existing structure. The Sapokka Water Garden, one result of this green policy, received several awards in the nineties. This helped the city gain wider public acclaim.

Involved Parties

The realization of the Katariina Beach Park would not have been possible without the perseverance of the Kotka municipal authorities, who have been pursuing an ambitious policy in the interests of greenery and nature spaces for two whole decades. In particular, the landscape architect Heikki Laaksonen, whose creative energy has been trans-

forming the city of Kotka since 1985, played an important role, as he ultimately directed the layout of Katariina Beach Park and led the design for Katariina Beach Park. The landscape gardener responsible for it was Tomi Uusitalo—who works for the company Pihat Oy Uusitalo. Savaterra Oy, a company that specializes in treating polluted soil as well as industrial and municipal waste—was appointed by the oil companies to clean up the site. The Southeastern Finnish Regional Center for the Environment (Kaakkois-Suomen Ympäristökeskus) supported the City of Kotka in this green project.

For some time now, the City of Kotka has been taking steps to have its network of green areas and nature spaces recognized by the Finnish Ministry of the Environment as a national city park (Kansallinen Kaupunkipuisto). This status, which has been their aim since the land use and building law came into force in 2000, is closely modeled after the Swedish model. A national city park can be created in order to protect and maintain the aesthetics of a cultural and natural landscape, historic features,

and the qualities of an urban area with regard to development, social aspects, and recreation. To this end, local authorities have to work out a land management plan in cooperation with the Regional Center for the Environment, which establishes an applicable maintenance framework and usage modalities for the areas in question.

This law recognizes as national city parks natural areas that preserve biodiversity in the urban environment, or that are open-air or built cultural sites of historical interest for the city or the countryside, as well as parks and greenery of high aesthetic value and design quality. Furthermore, these areas will contribute to ecological continuity by facilitating interaction with natural areas on the urban periphery. The City of Kotka is counting on its high-quality network of green areas and parks to achieve this recognition, which would honor initiatives carried out over the past two decades. This park project also operates as a means of pooling local resources to display the local wealth of green and natural areas.

St. Petersburg. Because of its more modern and dynamic face, entrepreneurs and investors are also discovering the city. Green areas or buildings with distinctive architecture have replaced the industrial wastelands symbolic of the poor economic climate from the late nineteen-eighties.

In 2012, the City of Kotka allocated about 3 million euros (0.8% of the municipal budget) to its Green Areas Department. Apart from the fact that these green areas provide its inhabitants amenities, this sum can also be regarded as a worthwhile investment in terms of improving the city's image.

Conclusion

It might seem paradoxical to establish a park on an industrial wasteland, considering the highly contaminated soil that made its transformation difficult. Furthermore, the hotel industry showed a strong interest in developing the southern tip of Kotka's central island. However, the very attitude to such challenges evidently contributed to the change of image and of mentalities. In this respect, the success of the City of Kotka with its parks and gardens can serve as an example for others, especially for those facing a decline of industrial activities that are detrimental to the environment.

With just a little over 50,000 inhabitants, today Kotka has become well known due to its green planning. Although the city has clearly become more attractive for tourists and investors, it is undoubtedly the local inhabitants who have benefited the most from this policy. They had suffered the most from economic decline and the accompanying stigmatization. The potential of green projects to change a region's perception functions as an important means of giving the area and its inhabitants new incentive, and generating secondary benefits for the economy and the city.

Financial Framework

The oil companies involved covered the 10-million-euro soil remediation costs. The City of Kotka invested around 1.2 million euros in the park's realization. The European Union contributed 121,000 euros to the project from its structural funds.

The image of the Kotka, a city that had been dominated by its industry and its oil ports, changed fundamentally. The local tourist information centers now advertise the attractive features of the park and the garden, especially to Russians visiting from

Germany
Finland
France
Netherlands
United
Kingdom

Lille Métropole
Parc de la Deûle

MURIEL DELABARRE

The Project's Innovative Aspects

The park was planned on a 350-hectare area along the Deûle Canal, in the gaps formed by industrial wasteland and the peripheral area of Lille. The idea of a wide green belt between the city of Lille and the coal basin of Lens had been suggested as early as 1960. In 1993, this proposal was finally carried out, as there were ever-louder calls for improving the living environment, protecting the natural environment, and better integrating agriculture. The project was officially given the go-ahead during the celebrations of Lille 2004, European Capital of Culture. Today a green network runs through this area, ensuring an ecological and natural connection between its various parts. The park received the French Landscape Award from the Ministry of the Environment in 2006 and the Landscape Award from the Council of Europe in 2009. These two awards undoubtedly contributed to raising awareness of the project. The Parc de la Deûle is currently regarded as a successful model for plotting metropolitan public spaces in a way that integrates neighboring agricultural enterprises and natural areas.

The park takes up the strong lines of the waterway network and the plot's design, as well as the geographical land formations. This green infrastructure was implemented along well-indicated walking paths, and it focuses on three different aspects of the landscape:

- "recovered nature": this aims to contribute to recovering industrial wastelands, restoring natural habitats, and upgrading existing wetland areas and the subsoil's ecological quality.
- "tamed nature": this aims to support agricultural areas by restoring meadows, hedges, and ditches, as well as a diverse agriculture and its products, including through their ecologically controlled cultivation.
- "dreamt nature": this aims to develop a green aesthetic via a botanical ornamental garden, which also provides a habitat for plants and animals.

The park provides various types of public greenery, such as a boulevard (Grande Allée de Wavrin) several hundred meters long, which now connects the city of Wavrin directly with the banks of the Deûle Canal, as well as with promenades traversing empty areas, forests, wet meadows, and fields. Elsewhere, the Mosaïc Garden, the centerpiece of the park, exhibits a series of themed spaces highlighting local rural traditions from the Lille area.

The landscape's overall structure ensures coherence between varied public green areas. The landscape architects Jacques Simon and Yves Hubert, who also served as the project's site managers, viewed the canal as a thread linking the park's various components. To this first axis they added a second, a winding watercourse that had previously formed a drainage system for agricultural water on the Deûle plain. Structuring connecting elements link all the planned sections of the park. They create interstitial relationships characterized by one of the three types of nature ("recovered", "tamed", or "dreamt") identified in the project. While laying out the natural scenery, the planners also took the rural and urban areas into account. Using a cooperative approach, they drew up a charter that integrates agriculture into the landscape project. This document sets out common criteria for coordinating various agricultural elements (stakes, fences, ditch bridges). The principles reinforce the project guidelines, which were worked out in a clear, processual procedure. The green area represents the first component of a metropolitan-level system, forming the basis for planning other parks. The landscape project makes it possible to consider the spatial layout on a broader level. The green network clearly delineates the natural structures (land formations and waterways) and the anthropogenic ones in order to bring clarity and consistency to Lille's new layout as a metropolis. The park presents a staging of nature that revolves around three different nature themes.

Involved Parties

As early as 1973, the City of Lille, as the client, had incorporated the idea of this green system in its guiding schematic (Schéma Directeur). Starting in 1993, the project was directed by a Parc de la Deûle municipal syndicate comprised of Lille Métropole and the municipalities of Wavrin, Houplin-Ancoisne, and Santes. Shortly thereafter, the organization contracted the team Simon & JNC International, which drew up the designs in 1995. The municipal syndicate also benefited from the technical competence of Lille's Metropolitan Natural Areas Department of the Office for Urban Planning and Development. This technical expertise, in conjunction with the planning of wider regional areas, gave the project significant advantages and led to its success and extension. A series of interviews with members of the local population who were involved (residents, farmers, nature re-

searchers, politicians) was another factor contributing to the project's success. As a result of these consultations, a metropolitan supervisory board was founded, which represents agricultural trade unions, nature conservation associations, outdoor sports clubs, and cultural societies. In 1997, the park became the main project of the Lille's development schematic. In February 1999, 277 hectares of land were allotted to public use, and the building work started.

The Parc de la Deûle forms part of the Green Metropolis (Métropole Verte) strategy. At the end of the nineteen-nineties, as part of the green development schematic, authorities proposed a project creating a wide green belt by linking extensive areas that hold ecological or recreational value. As part of a charter establishing objectives for this planning document and the Green Metropolis strategy, the City of Lille, the local authorities, the region, and the state all signed a declaration of commitment. One of its objectives was to establish over 10,000 hectares of natural and recreational areas within the Lille metropolitan region within ten years. The municipal syndicate Natural Areas Lille Métropole (Espace Naturel Lille Métropole) is responsible for implementing this extensive green infrastructure.

Financial Framework

Within ten years, 350 hectares and 40 kilometers of pathways were upgraded or created in the four main municipalities involved. The park's expansion to the north and south will ultimately link Lille to Lens, totaling 2,000 hectares of agricultural and natural areas. The idea of a green and blue network underlies this plan which also reveals the ambition to create a networked European landscape where ecotourism, ecology, and agriculture come together even within densely populated areas.

Conclusion

The Parc de la Deûle, which lies at the gateway to the city, satisfies an urban population's need for recreational spaces and fulfills the goal of providing a spacious natural area that is accessible to all. Although the park's users may not be aware of the specifics, the park's landscape applies its three guiding principles—"recovered", "tamed", and "dreamt nature"—to create a near-natural landscape that offers expressive scenes and settings: industrial wastelands, wetland areas, meadows, fields, hedges and ditches, gardens, yards, and pathways. The Parc de la Deûle plays a valuable structuring role within the urban region.

Lyon
Confluence

MURIEL DELABARRE

The Project's Innovative Aspects

Following the logic of inward urban regeneration, the Lyon Confluence project has repurposed a former industrial and logistics site. Currently in the process of being qualitatively upgraded and doubled in size, this redevelopment area in the south of the Lyon peninsula is a central area of the city.

In the first phase of the area's development (total area of 41.5 hectares), a city district with mixed functions will be created in the northern section along the Saône River. Arranged around a two-hectare lake, the combination of housing, offices, and public facilities aims for a heterogeneous inner-city character. A recreational and cultural center is to be built in the south, providing commercial and services functions. To the west, a city park borders the area.

In 2010, the second phase of the project began, linking the landscape and buildings over a total area of 35 hectares. Instead of a major market on the Rhône riverbank, a dense but permeable city district was planned. The new residential blocks are designed to be permeable to air and light. The combination of different building heights and types allows plenty of daylight into the interior courtyard gardens. This transparency also enables a tight cluster of trees to thrive, vegetation that further defines the character of the public space. To the south, a residential park, Le Champ, which means "the field", interrupts the dense city district. The park has been incorporated into the project's overall system, and it evokes the former winding landscape of the peninsula. In 2009, the Ministry of Ecology awarded the urban development project the "Palmarès des écoquartiers" Eco-district Prize in the category urban density and forms. What the jury appreciated most was the balance between dense residential blocks and the open park.

In 2000, the River Saône—a system of plant and water axes—was chosen as the heart of the park. The park itself was designed as a ramified, meandering system that winds along the riverbank and fills the spaces in between buildings of different types and densities. In total, the 14 hectare park has 3,280 tall trees. The design's aim is to create a landscape that appears natural.

The park's adaptability and flexibility are also characteristic of the development of the new city district. The concept of a "ramified park" is primarily based on the concept of closely interlinking nature and housing. Therefore plants and soils were selected that could adapt to water and buildings. The park, which had to meet certain technical and user requirements, consists of a combination of waterways (ditches, harbor basins, and water gardens). The new greenery references spatial traces of the past by reinterpreting the landscape.

The operation's extent enables a variety of natural forms:

• Vegetation as structuring element
The first phase of Lyon Confluence stipulated that the park's structure should continue along the streets into the heart of the development, a requirement that the landscape planner Michel Desvigne calls "Green Fingers". In the second phase of the project's implementation, the planted areas became particularly important; despite a high building density, stress was laid on incorporating garden courtyards and tree copses. The innovative design of the private areas also makes planting possible. Finally, this second phase of the project encompasses the creation of a new kind of park, called Le Champ, in the southernmost part of the area. This park, with a form that was new for Lyon, has trees lining water ditches that run through the whole park. Although private plots account for the largest proportion of the Le Champ project, there will also be an extensive public park in this area to ensure ecological diversity by providing a habitat for several dozen animal and plant species.

• Adding value to the waterways
Owing to floods, the Rhône and Saône Rivers were considered dangerous for a long time. Today, the access to the rivers within the city represents a new urban quality, and the area's natural heritage gains in value. A harbor basin is planned in the park center, allowing the water of the Saône to flow to the main artery Cours Charlemagne and enabling access to a river pier. This two-hectare basin also serves as an event venue. The water gardens that were planted on both sides of the basin complement the natural spaces provided for people strolling along the banks of the Saône. Meadows, pastures, forests, and aquatic plants form the nature complex. Only resilient plants were selected, because they can withstand Lyon's climate and need little maintenance. These water areas are designed as active ecosystems, with the wetland vegetation providing a habitat for ducks, dragonflies, and other wildlife. Waterways bring ecological diversity into the city and strengthen the extension and application of the ecological principle.

• The reinforced green and blue network
On a broader level, the networks of these water-ways become even clearer: the Balmes de Sainte-Foy-lès-Lyon on the right bank of the Saône and the Parc de Gerland on the Rhône. The project envisages a "blue network" around the Rhône and the Saône and a "green network" along the river-banks. A tree-lined pedestrian and cycle path are planned along the rivers.

This nature project is strongly oriented towards the American park system from the nineteenth century, which often served as a structuring element for a city's growth. The parks by Frederick Law Olmsted in Minneapolis and Boston, which add value to cities that do not enjoy an advantageous geo-graphical location, convinced the design teams to pay attention to the clues the landscape provided. In the spatial design of Lyon Confluence, one can observe an aesthetic derived from traces of the past; relics of the local geography, a series of infra-structures, and former industrial sites provided op-portunities to reconquer and regenerate this area.

Involved Parties
The project is carried out by a partnership called the Société Publique Locale d'Aménagement (SPLA). The SPLA Lyon Confluence aims to imple-ment spatial planning measures and programs in this area. It is responsible for carrying out project studies, purchasing land, managing the public spaces, selling plots to private developers, and overseeing construction, agreements, and com-munication.

In 2000, the construction management team for the first phase, consisting of the city plan-ner François Grether and the landscape archi-tect Michel Desvigne, started their work on this project. Since 2002, the planning office Tribu has supported the SPLA as the building consultant for sustainable development aspects. The planning of-fice had the responsibility of drawing up regulations that apply to the entire urban development proj-ect. In 2007, this sustainability perspective played an even more important role, because before the start of the second phase (Rhône), a sustainability

assessment had to be compiled. The project planning documentation recorded its conclusions. Subsequently, the planner proposed an innovative approach to implementing the development project. He directed the cooperation between five complementary divisions:

- The Divison for City Planning, Landscape, and Architecture: Herzog & de Meuron (city planning) and Michel Desvigne (landscape design)
- The Division for Program Planning and Agreements: Initial Consultants and Sémaphores

- The Division for Streets, Supply Networks, and Mobility: Opus, Girus, Item
- The Division for Sustainable Development: Tribu
- The Division for Polluted Areas and Soil: Sogreah Magelis

All of these divisions took account of the sustainability recommendations that form the heart of the overall identity of Lyon Confluence. The Lyon Confluence project was realized within the wider context of "Grand Lyon," which defines its overall approach in the local Agenda 21 and through its

gram's objective—which has previously been test-ed only in new projects (for example, Bedzed in the south of London, Masdar in Abu Dhabi, the tourist complex Mata de Sesimbra in Portugal)—is to re-duce our ecological footprint (with regard to energy, water, waste, biodiversity) and to refrain from caus-ing new greenhouse gas emissions until 2020.

Financial Framework

From 2003 to 2016, 177 million euros were invested as part of the public planning act. In 2006, the first construction phase began, spanning 41 hectares (40% of the total project area). The decision-makers found the convenient location appealing, as well as the new facilities and a 250,000-square-meter area dedicated to the service sector. The project attracted major corporations such as Eiffage, GDF Suez, Cardinal, and GL Events, which established its headquarters here. The administrative head-quarters for the Rhône-Alpes region are also in this district. By 2014, a total of almost 7,000 adminis-trators had settled in Lyon Confluence. The proj-ect benefits from the appeal of its recreational and commercial center by Unibail-Rodamco, as well as from its green residential blocks, which were de-signed by twelve famous architecture teams spe-cifically to attract decision-makers and investors. Thus far 1.5 billion euros have been invested, and 64% of this has come from private sources.

Conclusion

The urban development project focuses on traces of the past and the degraded landscape. Instead of filling the empty spaces with new structures, the project creates a new geography using simple means: marking traces of the original landscape, taking soil fertility into account, providing drainage for rainwater, and setting up an innovative manage-ment procedure for maintenance. The first phase of the creation of public spaces has formed prototypes that will be extended across the whole area. The interconnected spatial measures ultimately form a continuity in the landscape, which the natural world reflects (plants, water, biodiversity, soil, sky, and sun). The implemented spatial configurations (such as the harbor basin and the water gardens) or those that are still in progress (such as Le Champ) are not only designed to structure the urban and natural material development. By increasing the residential plots' value, they also have considerable impact on housing types.

local action plans. As set out in the urban area's climate plan, this project contributes, for example, to the incorporation of plants into the urban en-vironment, in accordance with the so-called tree charter, as well as to the drainage of rainwater on building plots, the sanitation of polluted sites and soil, and the attempted reduction of greenhouse gas emissions, in accordance with Factor Four for Horizon 2050.

It is the first sustainable city district in France aligned with the guidelines of the World Wildlife Fund's concept of "One Planet Living." This pro-

Germany
Finland
France
Netherlands
United
Kingdom

Breda
Au Fil de l'Eau

JENNIFER BUYCK

The Project's Innovative Aspects

Breda, the former capital of the province Noord Brabant, currently has about 172,000 inhabitants. For thirty years, the city has been pursuing sustainable urban development in order to distinguish itself from its neighbors Rotterdam and Amsterdam. Its urban development approaches, which are both environmentally friendly and social, are regarded as exemplary among medium-sized European cities.

Using past and present synergies in the areas of urbanity, landscape, quality of life, qualitative architectural design, soft mobility, and open-space planning, the city is distinguished by the following global and integrative approaches:

- Creation of energy balance
- Reduction of sources of waste and smells
- Increased biodiversity
- Urban development based on existing canals and rivers
- Rainwater management
- Preservation of public quiet zones, as a contrast to a dynamic way of life
- Connections between outdoor spaces within the city (Green Fingers generally accessible within 200 meters)
- Economic projects for environmental sustainability

The objective of these approaches, which are applicable across the board—urban region, municipality, and district—is to increase the city's appeal and to help control the suburbanization process. The city is less concerned with enhancing its image through exceptional architecture and more with developing the city in a sustainable, long-term manner and upgrading its components. The urban planning also adheres to a so-called care policy. Instead of merely advancing visionary ideas, the project aims to improve the quality of life by establishing a new, shared urbanity; raising civic awareness of matters such as open space, nature, and community awareness; and boosting local (political) participation.

Due to the high flood risk posed by the many rivers and canals, the City of Breda is pursuing two goals: developing an integrated rainwater management system and protecting water retention zones. The City of Breda has set up a flood protection system. Seeking the watercourses' renaturation, the plan has proposed laying down meanders and redirecting river courses into their original riverbeds. This procedure helps protect existing ecosystems and green urban spaces.

By establishing pedestrian and cycle path connections in the water retention zones, the plan seeks to offer cyclists and pedestrians new options. One of the open space projects, for example, uncovers a previously canalized river course in the city center.

Involved Parties

The project brings together a number of parties, including experts and local politicians, who have dedicated themselves to its long-term success. This continuity has withstood political changes. Creating a common basis requires a variety of perspectives and measures: putting together a professional city plan, considering the flow of mobility, designing the public space, focusing on the city center, and building new districts.

The City of Breda plays a major role in the project's governance and thereby ensures cohesion among all parties. Furthermore, the various integrated water management measures the City has taken have resulted in a wide range of technical alternatives for rainwater usage:

- Drains that channel rainwater into the canals
- New drainage systems
- Ground and surface permeability
- New vegetation along waterways and canals
- Basins with greenery
- Water reservoirs

With regard to architecture and urban planning, Breda's development is future-oriented. The ideas for new peripheral city districts, which bring together past and present, are especially valuable. The qualitative standards do not apply only to a few pilot projects, but also serve an important function in planning open public spaces.

Financial Framework

The success of Breda's sustainable urban development policy can in large part be attributed to cooperation in the form of a public-private partnership (PPP). There is no ideal city size for realizing this type of project. Success depends more on the ambitions and initiatives of the involved parties, and on their ability to reflect on their actions. These qualities are an important basis for innovation and creativity. Furthermore, cooperation in the form of a PPP requires input and capital from at least two parties. In this case, it creates a win-win situation that sustains the project over the long term and adapts it to the local situation.

The City of Breda is pursuing soft urban development with a view to sustainability. Concrete objectives include the following: creating targeted connections between densely built-up areas and open spaces, requiring a basic level of architectural quality, integrating social aspects, advancing "soft" (low in CO_2) forms of mobility, creating public spaces that serve as quiet zones, and offering the city's inhabitants recreational and cultural facilities. The requirement for sustainability does not, however, stand in the way of the city's economic development. Breda proves that sustainability and social, economic dynamism are not mutually exclusive.

An interesting example is the casino in Breda, which is housed in a sixteenth-century monastery. The city sold it to a private investor for one forint under the condition that the buyer would renovate the listed building. This contractual measure was the only way to rescue this city monument from decline, and at the same time it set in motion an economic development that now attracts 650,000 visitors a year to Breda.

Conclusion

Breda, the Netherlands' ninth largest city, is one of a series of medium-sized cities that lie between two major attractive urban centers, Antwerp and Rotterdam. Consequently, Breda suffers severe air pollution coming from Rotterdam, Antwerp, the Ruhr area, and even from England. Breda has few attractions itself, apart from a handful of historical monuments, but they cannot compete with those in Amsterdam or Delft.

Despite these difficulties, Breda has to be able to develop further by encouraging innovation and protecting itself against negative environmental influences. Breda is seeking to stabilize or even increase the number of inhabitants by developing efficient public transport systems and alternative energy solutions. In order to distinguish itself

from Rotterdam and not be regarded as its suburb, Breda is investing in autonomy, good accessibility, a high quality of life, and a variety of cultural and commercial facilities.

It is not just the uniformity of Breda's architecture that surprises the viewer, but also its unusual living environments, such as long balconies protruding over the canal, ecological districts, and canals with incredibly lush vegetation. This creates livable and distinctive city districts without vanity or provocation. These unusual living environments stem from a conventional urban situation that gains individuality through its unique relationship to nature. The relationship between city and nature also plays an important role on a regional level, especially with regard to the problems of suburbanization.

The planning policy of Breda also stands out. It focuses on the nature of boundaries and borders: on the one hand, the state-prescribed settlement boundaries and, on the other, the self-determined borders with natural areas. In the Netherlands, these consist of artificially created polders and cultivated areas for agriculture. The self-determined nature of these borders enables both "nature" and "city" to be continuously redesigned.

In this cultural context, the Breda Municipal Council has two main interests. The first is keeping agriculture within its designated territory. Second, it aims to achieve a mutually profitable relationship between farmers' requirements and those of urbanites. Although the urbanization boundaries are strictly defined to prevent urban sprawl, there are still many opportunities for dialogue between the city and nature: canal banks, planted noise protection walls, green corridors, and green areas in urban neighborhoods. This openness towards greenery and nature represents sought-after capital to investors, who see it as increasing the value of their local projects.

Amsterdam
Borneo & Sporenburg

JENNIFER BUYCK

The Project's Innovative Aspects

Amsterdam, as the capital and the largest city of the Netherlands, is also its economic and cultural center. The city was built at the end of the twelfth century around a semicircular canal system. Since then, it has developed along the estuary of the Amstel River. The historical center of Amsterdam currently has more than 700,000 inhabitants and a density of 33.6 inhabitants per hectare. The agglomeration of Amsterdam has about 2.3 million inhabitants, representing a density of eighteen inhabitants per hectare. It is not easy to reconcile this high population density with a high quality of life. In this context, the restructuring of the islands Borneo and Sporenburg serves as an important example of new developments in Amsterdam that combine risk management and environmental improvement.

The first development plan in Amsterdam to gain international acclaim was the Algemeen Uitbreidingsplan (AUP), the General Urban Expansion Plan, published in 1935. This plan set out a framework for the city's growth through the year 2000 and was the basis for its spatial development in the nineteen-seventies. Since then, many development plans have followed, responding to the city's new spatial and social requirements.

From 1980 to 1990, inhabitants and companies relocated from the city center to satellite towns. The so-called compact city plan in 1985 sought to curb this urban expansion. Since the nineteen-nineties, Amsterdam's urban population has increased again, and many companies have established themselves there. The city and its surroundings form a network of cities and an urban region.

Since 1991, additional plans have been drawn up that address the question of the environment. In 2003, Amsterdam put forward a new urban development plan called Choose Urbanity. It aimed to use the city's built-up areas more intensively, creating more space for living and working in the same city by applying two concepts: "trading spaces" (areas for trading products, information, and services; and "meeting spaces" (areas for meeting others). As part of this, the regeneration of the Eastern Dock stands out as the best example of transforming a nineteenth-century industrial quarter into a contemporary residential district. The restructuring program encompasses 8,000 housing units for 17,000 inhabitants as well as retail and trade units. By combining social housing, rental housing, and purchased property, this project prioritized social mixing. The most significant parts of this project are located on the islands of Sporenburg and Borneo.

Two other peninsulas (Java and KNSM) had already been restructured at an earlier point. Although the planning of Java and KNSM bears similarities to Sporenburg and Borneo, they have a different configuration. On Java and KNSM, the development consists of a mass of individual and connected tall buildings. On Borneo and Sporenburg, in contrast, there are layers of low buildings that highlight the landscape. Furthermore, tall, artistically designed blocks are used as an accent set off against the horizon (see diagram).

Here we can see a new typology, in an extremely horizontal form, based on the concept of hyperdensity: a fabric woven out of individual and row houses, lined up along straight streets as a homogeneous development, revealing the signature of the most renowned architects, parallel to quiet waterways with docks. "It is the brainchild of the landscape planner Adriaan Geuze, who drew up the master plan and the architectural guidelines (…)." ("Hyperdensity in Borneo Sporenburg", in: Lotus n°108/2001, pp. 39–45).

Involved Parties

The old harbor area east of the docks, near the heart of Amsterdam, became the focus of several projects. Each dock was assigned to an architect. Jo Coenen was assigned the island KNSM and applied a relatively conventional planning concept. Sjoerd Soeters planned the island of Java using a postmodern concept, and Adriaan Geuze (West 8) was interested in Borneo and Sporenburg, applying a concept that integrates the urban landscape.

West 8, a group of Dutch architects, won the competition for restructuring the islands of Borneo and Sporenburg in the Eastern Docklands Area of Amsterdam. Between 1992 and 2000, they converted an unused harbor zone into a new district with 2,500 individual housing units and communal residential blocks. The overarching responsibility lay with NEX Deal BV, while another architect realized each housing unit.

After years of researching how suburban areas along the Ijsselmeer develop, the City of Amsterdam was seeking space for its urban growth. The government started first with building on ground that had formerly been used for container storage, warehouses, and rail tracks. The names of the islands of Borneo and Sporenburg derive from their former functions: the Borneo peninsula was the port that received goods from the Indonesian island of the same name, and the name Sporenburg refers to the railroad tracks—sporen in Dutch.

Their location in the middle of Amsterdam Harbor gives these two new city districts a waterside urbanity, allowing the sea to enter into a dialogue with the city here. Blind façades on the ground floor, higher entrances, and watertight sealing systems all reduce the risk of flooding. These measures, which are common in the Netherlands, are, however, sometimes in conflict with the legal policies for flood risk management.

Financial Framework
The origins of the new Borneo-Sporenburg district go back to before the Dutch VINEX residential building program began in 1993. To a certain extent, this project was a precursor of current residential building policy, and it set a new benchmark back then.

The program's financial framework reflects current influential factors in the Netherlands: the agreement with regard to the plot's size (a VINEX preliminary agreement), the housing use (policy of property purchase and social mixing), the financing (profit-based ways of using sites), and the involved parties (authorities and partnerships). The municipal administration has little influence on this development. Evidently, social and cultural context largely determine the development of residential areas in the Netherlands. Even though the economic and political context dictates the forms administration and financing take, the predominant policy encourages social mixing. Adriaan Geuze (West 8), who designed the urban development and master plans for one aspect of this project, proposed dense duplex housing in order to meet the great demand for single-family housing, while still achieving a profitable use of the plots. A total of 2,500 housing units form a dense network (100 units per hectare), which is punctuated by occasional taller elements. In order to reconcile the need for density with single-family housing, Adriaan Geuze in-

vented new typologies of residential blocks, thereby radically re-envisioning the Dutch row house. Public space on the street is reduced. The houses with three floors and a roof terrace also have private gardens that become separate terraces or interior courtyards; this design, despite its compactness, preserves permeability in and transparency of the urban fabric.

These buildings have a particular relationship to the water, whose level is just a few centimeters below the ground floor. Thus, the built-up area and the environment mutually benefit each other.

Conclusion

The structure of the old docks has been preserved and combined with a series of identical modules, individual and striking houses, private gardens, and green areas. This has led to a new, open city district, which is integrated into its natural surroundings despite its high density; overall, this creates an impression of continuity in greenery and high-quality public spaces.

The houses are accessed directly from the street without any transition. The minimization of public space allows for a maximum of individual, private space. There are no semipublic spaces, no obstacles, and no greenery on the street. Apart from the house's front door, there are no thresholds. As soon as one leaves the house, one encounters public space. The repetition of single-family homes within a broader structure reflects the pattern of the docks.

The omnipresence of water counterbalances the island's population density, and gives the "water city" a familiar and simultaneously exciting atmosphere. 50% of each plot is used as private gardens or interior courtyards, so a concealed area lies behind each house's façade.

For a long time, development in Amsterdam has focused on creating artificial islands. In this particular

case, the islands were formed by dredging sand (the so-called pancake method). The ground level of the islands lies one to two meters above sea level.

An ambitious ecological plan seeks to minimize the extreme density's negative effects on the eco-system, in particular by creating a mosaic of green islands forming an ecological corridor.

The Eastern Docks Quarter bears a uniform de-sign, while nevertheless making a variegated im-pression. A list of unifying requirements drawn up by the architects makes this possible:

- uniform use of material (bricks and wood)
- variations in the openings, which vary through an interplay of modules yet still form a series
- new types of houses with three floors of varied layouts, which are based on traditional Dutch building dimensions
- a construction principle that favors a street-facing façade with direct access and an on-site garage: in addition, each house has an interior space of double height, and an interior courtyard and/or garden

At three points, higher residential buildings inter-rupt the rhythm of the three-floor houses. These artistically designed blocks act as marker posts within the urban landscape: the Fountainhead by Steven Holl, the Walyis by Architekten Cie, and the Pacman by Koen van Velsen. They refer to other large buildings in Amsterdam, visually integrate the landscape into the city, and, at the same time, open the city up to the landscape. Retail spaces and restaurants occupy most ground floors and in-terior courtyards, forming semipublic spaces.

Germany
Finland
France
Netherlands
**United
Kingdom**

East London
Green Grid

CHARLES AMBROSINO

The Project's Innovative Aspects

The East London Green Grid forms the framework for green infrastructure in the East London region. More broadly, the Grid also functions within the city's urban development program, and it serves as part of the Thames Gateway Parklands Spatial Framework, which aims to improve the region's living conditions. It represents the largest regeneration scheme in Great Britain. Encompassing an extensive transregional area, it stretches downstream along both banks of the Thames through the three counties of London, Kent, and Essex. This area, which has two million inhabitants, faces some of the United Kingdom's most challenging problems (unemployment, poverty, soil pollution, and poor accessibility). The green infrastructure's design not only links various natural or planted areas, but also lends the urban areas a coherent structure. It is also intended to contribute to overcoming various environmental challenges, such as flooding and climate change.

The East London Green Grid is divided into six interconnected sub-districts. Strategic green corridors link town centers and transport hubs to the most important employment centers and large residential areas. The river courses, their banks, and connections to the green belt are all central elements of the project. The way this infrastructure is formed points to the fractal character of the London region and, on a wider scale, of southeast England. This brings to mind Richard Rogers's or Bernardo Secchi's comments about the creative power inherent to open spaces. In contrary to a city characterized by its mobile urban population's individualistic attitudes to transport, this project puts forward a green infrastructure that binds the city's disparate elements.

Involved Parties

A partnership structure, the East London Green Grid Project Board, is in charge of implementing the East London Green Grid project. Its members include the following entities:

- The London Development Agency (the development division for Greater London)
- The Department for Communities and Local Government
- The ten East London boroughs covered by the Green Grid
- The Thames Gateway London Partnership
- Thames Gateway delivery vehicles
- The Environment Agency
- Natural England

The East London Green Grid is based on a general vision rather than a normative one. The overall vision promotes decentralized

planning and individual management that is adapted to local priorities and strategies. The vision is based on two documents published by London Plan (a planning body for Greater London):

- The "East London Green Grid Primer" (a plan that serves communication purposes and was published in 2006)
- The "East London Green Grid Framework Supplementary Planning Guidance" (a planning document first published in 2008 and updated several times)

The second document drawn up for Greater London—the Supplementary Planning Guidance (SPG)—places the East London Green Grid within an interregional framework. It provides guidelines for local city planning documents, such as local development frameworks, open space strategies, regeneration frameworks, master plans, or building applications.

- This guideline is important to the vision's realization. Among other things, it ensures the participation of the ten involved London boroughs. The borough of Tower Hamlets, for example, aims to develop a Green Grid and has stated this as part of its core strategy in its "Key Spatial Themes" document.
- The guideline also proposes that joint development plan documents or area action plans be drawn up for all six boroughs covered in the East London Green Grid. These measures are designed to safeguard biodiversity, as well as to improve accessibility, interconnection, and quality of the parks, the recreational areas, open spaces, and rivers. A local president and a management committee share responsibility for each of the six areas incorporated into the grid.

Financial Framework

The fruition of the Green Grid's preliminary scheme is expected to take at least twenty-five years and requires an investment of more than half a billion pounds, of which 80 million has already been raised. Around 300 projects have been selected, seventy of which the London Development Agency has supported and designated as priorities on the basis of feasibility. The projects that are the easiest to realize are those that build on an existing management system and local direction. Large projects also play an important role, especially for securing substantial investments. The Erith Marshes and

Belvedere Links Project, along the Thames in the borough of Bexley, aims to transform one of the largest former industrial zones into a long-term employment center. The project was established to reduce flood risk, to improve the Erith wetland environment, and to create 5,000 to 10,000 new local jobs. The key measures are upgrading the dam network and creating publicly accessible spaces, developing sustainable drainage systems, and improving pedestrian and cycle paths. The Communities and Local Governments Parklands Program and the European Regional Development Fund have raised around 10.6 million pounds. In addition, the London Development Agency has contributed two million pounds.

Special Features

An analysis of the East London Green Grid reveals current strategic planning trends. This project is based on the idea that green spatial elements can shape the city's in-between areas. It uses open spaces as a structure to serve functions previously fulfilled by the modern city's street networks. Furthermore, the implementation of the East London Green Grid reflects a search for the right scale for developing metropolitan regions. The new, green infrastructural elements will provide spatial coherence. Generally speaking, the project of the contemporary city is one that is primarily rooted in the ground and gives purpose and structure to a disparate, fragmented, and diverse agglomeration. This new type of green project creates a link between various

city regions. Empty areas are revalorized and given meaning within an overall green plan. This structure creates locations with a new urban aesthetic.

The initiative combines different political arenas and therefore serves as an invitation to reconsider classic modes of governmental leadership. The project's central concern is to safeguard long-term investments that extend beyond its launch. The matter of long-term management is key in this respect, especially in the context of limited competences and resources. Consequently, the local authorities cannot carry the burden alone. While drawing up the Supplementary Planning Guidance document, the Greater London Authority recognized this, and thus prioritized securing long-term financing for each project from the outset. The Supplementary Plan-

ning Guidance recommends incorporating the East London Green Grid into local budget planning and development guidelines, so that local authorities will be better positioned in the future to help project investors realize, improve, and manage the East London Green Grid project. The future maintenance costs should also be included in the plan from the beginning. This anticipatory planning before the project starts is a prerequisite for securing financial resources through the Greater London Authority.

London
Greenwich
Millennium
Village

The Project's Innovative Aspects

The Greenwich Millennium Village on the Greenwich Peninsula in London is the largest sustainable city planning project in the United Kingdom (thirty hectares) and is viewed nationwide as a model for ecological building. The Swedish architect Ralph Erskine designed its master plan and planned the construction of the first housing section. Each section is arranged around what appears to be a version of London Square and is surrounded by a thirteen-hectare green centerpiece with two artificial lakes and an eco-park. Green corridors and nature walks link the project to the Thames and the rest of the peninsula. 10,000 trees, bushes, and new grass landscapes were planted on this land of former pastures and ponds. This wide, open, and central space fulfills a variety of functions, such as public gardens, recreational areas, and places for ecological education and for environmental awareness-raising among adults and children alike. Reed beds and small islands were re-established to attract birds and provide them a protected habitat. In addition, 11 million pounds were invested to improve the Thames mud flats through an innovative system of riverbank terraces.

The Greenwich Peninsula, one of London's major industrial wastelands, is on the verge of regeneration. Located east of the Docklands, it was the former 121-hectare site of British Gas's operations plant. Thanks to its central location by the Thames, it offers strong development potential for business and residential purposes, as well as tourism. Furthermore, the peninsula has now been labeled one of the most important Opportunity Areas in the London Plan, an area development strategy for Greater London. By 2016, 16,000 jobs will be created and 7,500 housing units will be built here. The guidelines for regenerating the peninsula were set out as part of a broader urban development project called Thames Gateway. The project had to go through several phases before regional planning authorities approved the peninsula as a suitable area for sustainable urban development. The authorities' hesitation can be explained by, among other things, the considerable costs of soil remediation, the area's geographical isolation, and its poor transportation infrastructure.

Landscape Concept, Greenwich Millenium Village Design Code
Meridian Delta Limited (2004)
Greenwich Millennium Village Design Code, p. 24 /
© Erskine Tovatt Arkitekter AB

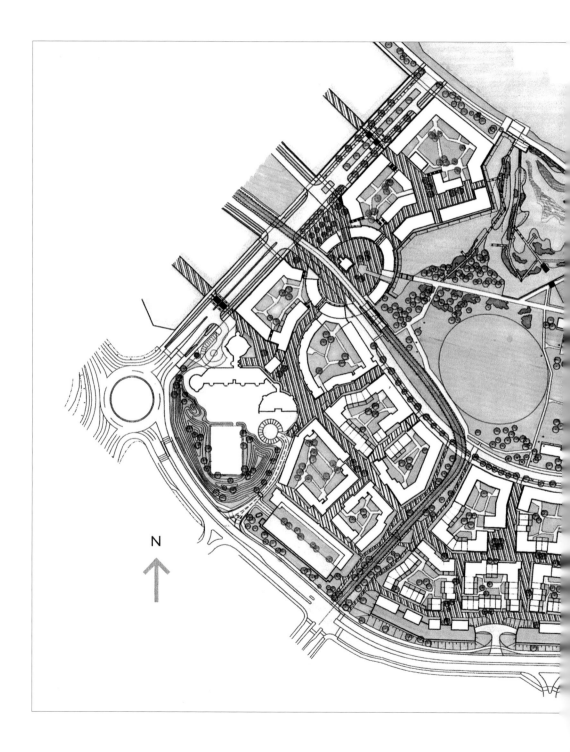

N

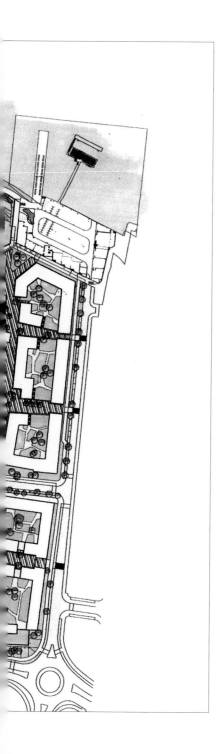

The Millennium Village in the southeast of the peninsula is one of the most important urban development projects. The developers of the new city district, Taylor Woodrow and Countryside Properties PLC, were selected in 1997 as a result of a Europe-wide competition. This competition was part of the Millennium Communities Program sponsored by English Partnerships, with the participation of the National Urban Regeneration Agency and the landowner. The selection criteria were the quality of the architecture and landscape design, as well as financial viability. On the heels of the competition, Greenwich Millennium Village Ltd was founded, which cooperates with the social housing partners Moat Housing Group and Ujima Housing.

The housing designed by Ralph Erskine promotes energy efficiency and social mixing. The village will have around 2,520 housing units in the form of residential complexes and town houses, of which 20% will be designated affordable housing. The buildings are arranged in a way that maximizes wind and sun exposure, and thus optimizes heating, hot water, and electricity consumption. The development guidelines stipulate a significant reduction in energy consumption (80%), which will be achieved by using energy-efficient materials and appliances. In addition to housing, Greenwich Millennium Village Ltd. funded a range of public facilities (school buildings and health complexes, as well as public spaces for the village and a riverbank promenade along the Thames.

Involved Parties

Ralph Erskine was commissioned by Taylor Woodrow and Countryside Properties PLC to draw up detailed project design guidelines, called the Greenwich Millennium Village Master Plan Design Code. Its purpose was to bring all involved parties together to work towards a clear design vision. The Design Code articulates key strategies for city planning and landscape conceptualization, which are open-ended enough to allow future negotiation with construction firms.

• The city planning strategies:
the Design Code differentiates between spatial sequences. In doing so, it aims to establish a hierarchy that defines various spaces by their different functions. The document identifies four types of space: the central park, the communications and transport axes, the public squares, and the residential-block interior courtyards with both

semiprivate and semipublic areas. The purpose is to enable better usage mixing in the urban area.

- The landscape planning strategies:
the Design Code helps clarify the status of spaces and promote urban diversity. It identifies five types of spaces: oval squares, community squares and spaces, spine streets, side streets, and courtyards. It makes recommendations for each type of sequence with regard to plants, land use, lighting, and street furniture; it clarifies these with plans, cross-sections, and references.

Financial Framework

Since 2002, the Trust for Urban Ecology (TRUE) has been responsible for the overall management of the Greenwich Peninsula Ecology Park, formerly owned by English Partnerships. This trust funds two full-time managers for this park. TRUE is a sub-department for urban ecology in the organization The Conservation Volunteers (TCV), which plays an important role in the ecological field and in the preservation of environmental heritage. TRUE has set out the following management principles for its parks:

- Urban fauna should form new habitats
- The park should raise awareness of urban ecology
- City residents, especially schoolchildren, should be given the opportunity to enjoy nature and to become familiar with it through practical experimentation
- The park should demonstrate "creative maintenance" as an ecological approach to creating new landscapes.

Conclusion

The Greenwich Millennium Village project came together successfully because of its planners' functional understanding of urban nature and their use of fairly traditional and sustainable city-planning objectives. Energy efficiency in the housing design ensures the area will have a smart ecology, as does the creation of open spaces, which improve the peninsula's layout and protect the flora and fauna along the Thames.

To a greater extent than elsewhere in London, nature plays an important role in this urban density project: it leads to further social acceptance of these apartment buildings and residential blocks in a country where these housing typologies have traditionally been culturally looked down upon. On

the municipal level, the Ecology Park assists in structuring the environment and forms part of the East London Green Grid. The park management's social strategy—as well as the type of activities offered and its aesthetic qualities—serve to make the Ecology Park a place where individuals experience new things and learn from them. The project combines raising awareness of nature with communicating ecological themes, which not only has a positive influence on its landscape planning and its ecological value, but also makes it innovative.

Greenery in the City
City by the Water

The traditional role of urban greenery is changing and expanding. Green areas are no longer merely aesthetic elements for embellishing cities. In the studied case examples, greenery also takes on many new spatial and social structuring functions. The evaluation of written research, surveys among those involved, and project analyses with regard to the ten cases presented here have led to the following five central insights:

Greenery becomes a spatial structuring element in city and regional planning

In an urban context, linking fragmented regional green areas establishes a new spatial order and orientation. In the British projects East London Green Grid and Greenwich Millennium Village, the diversity of green residual areas serves as a starting point for forming a new network that links previously unconnected urban areas physically and conceptually into one cohesive territory. A planning concept that takes all spatial scales (macro, meso, micro) into consideration in an interactive manner and makes new connections also influences how the project's planning is scheduled. A forward-thinking, open approach and an awareness of how to anticipate changes can bring forth sustainable, long-term development.

Greenery functions as a vector for integrative governance

Communication between politicians, experts, and end users (residents, citizens, visitors, interested parties) forms an important precondition to achieve widespread acceptance for the plan; communication also facilitates understanding of the particular usage forms and maintenance requirements. In the case of the Stuttgart Regional Landscape Park, for example, new legal directives paved the way. The Baden-Württemberg region allowed the municipalities involved to join together as the Stuttgart Regional Association. This newly established regional parliament grants citizens a greater legitimacy, and at the same time opens up possibilities for integrated planning (workshops, focus groups, trial plans). An open-ended dialogue—as well as the targeted, combined use of formal and informal participation—contributes significantly to the acceptance and long-term utilization of green projects.

Greenery attracts other amenities

Debates about sustainable urban development have led to a plethora of new types and functions of urban greenery. Green areas and vegetation that have a technical ecological function (water management, climate protection, ground mainte-nance) can also offer spaces and materials that visitors find appealing. As experienced in the city of Breda in the Netherlands and the city of Kotka in Finland, conventional green spaces appeal to investors, who view them as enhancing an area's value—especially in regards to the perception and appropriation of green border areas between the city and industry, as well as between the city and its surroundings. The multifunctional character of urban ecological green elements influences how one lives within the city and uses its spaces. The newly created green areas enhance the city in ways that can attract investors and new residents.

Greenery encourages new forms of local economy

Green flagship projects, such as Kotka in Finland and Sporenburg in the Netherlands, can be important driving forces for revitalizing the local economy; they can significantly increase a location's appeal, especially for potential investors. Furthermore, small-scale, progressive approaches to creating greenery, such as in Leipzig and Lille, can change a district's image and residents' and visitors' perceptions, and spur local economic development. A green policy can help establish new forms of local economy with financing that is more anticipatory and cooperative.

Germany
Stuttgart Region

Stuttgart Regional Association: Conference document No. 140/ 2004, Stuttgart 21.07.2004

Stuttgart Regional Association: Conference document No. 24/ 2005, Stuttgart 27.04.2005

Stuttgart Regional Association: Conference document No. 639/ 2008, Stuttgart 12.11.2008

Stuttgart Regional Association: Conference document No. 113/ 2010, Stuttgart 07.09.2010

Stuttgart Regional Association – public law authority: The Landscape Parks in the Stuttgart Region: http://www.landschaftspark-region-stuttgart.de, 22.09.2014

http://www.region-stuttgart.org/fileadmin/regionstuttgart/04_ Informationen_und_Download/04_01_Veroeffentlichungen/04_04_01_Broschueren_und_Faltblaetter/landschaftspark_ neckar_d.pdf, 22.09.2014»

http://www.region-stuttgart.org/fileadmin/regionstuttgart/04_ Informationen_und_Download/04_01_Veroeffentlichungen/04_04_01_Broschueren_und_Faltblaetter/landschaftspark_ rems.pdf, 22.09.2014»?

http://www.region-stuttgart.org/fileadmin/regionstuttgart/04_ Informationen_und_Download/04_01_Veroeffentlichungen/04_04_01_Broschueren_und_Faltblaetter/VRS_Landschaftspark_Albtrauf_Freigabe.pdf, 22.09.2014»

District by the Weiße Elster and the Karl Heine Canal, Leipzig

City of Leipzig Department of Urban Development and Construction (Ed.): Conceptional District Plan for the West of Leipzig (KSP West), "Contributions on Urban Development," Vol. 44, pp. 1–54

City of Leipzig: Forum Leipziger Westen: http://www.leipziger-westen.de/front_content.php?idart=225, 22.09.2014

City of Leipzig: Fördergebiete Leipziger Westen. http://www.leipzig.de/bauen-und-wohnen/foerdergebiete/leipziger-westen/efre-leipziger-westen, 17.11.2014)

We would like to thank the following people:

Mr. Manfred Meister from the Stuttgart Regional Association,

Ms. Elke Horstmann, City of Leipzig, City Planning Office – Planning Division West

Finland
Helsinki

Eronen, Matti: "The Green Fingers of Helsinki in Finland – A Green Structure as a Part of Master Planning," in Werquin, Ann Caroll et al., Green Structure and Urban Planning, Luxemburg 2005, pp. 352–358

Gordon, Douglas: "Helsinki, City" & "Helsinki, City-Region", in Douglas Gordon (Ed.), Polymetrex North-South Interface, http://www.eurometrex.org/Docs/PolyMetreX/rina/rina18/en_helSlnkl_north-South_flnal.pdf, Helsinki 2007, pp. 11–44

Gordon, Douglas/ Manninen, Rikhard/ Veltheim, Olavi (Ed.): From City to City-Region – City of Helsinki Strategic Spatial Plan, http://www.hel.fi/hel2/ksv/julkaisut/julk_2009-8.pdf, Helsinki 2009

Hannikainen, Matti O.: Classification of Green Spaces in Helsinki and Vantaa, Full Report of the "Green Issues Project", http:// greenspaceissues.files.wordpress.com/2013/03/greenspace-hannikainen.pdf, Helsinki 2013

Helsinki City Planning Department & Environmental Office: Green areas system in Helsinki http://www.kirjavasatama.fi/pdf/southharbour_greenareas- system_helsinki.pdf, Helsinki 2002

Huhdanmaki, Aimo/ Dubois-Taine, Geneviève: "Extension of Helsinki Region – Inner City, Edge City, Outskirts" in Geneviève Dubois-Taine (Ed.), European Cities: Insights on Outskirts – From Helsinki to Nicosia, Paris, 2004, pp. 97–121

Jaakkola, Marie: "Helsinki, Finland: Greenness and Urban Form", in Beatley, Timothy (Ed.), Green Cities of Europe – Global Lessons on Green Urbanism, Washington, DC 2012, pp. 109–128

Michalek, Michael: Helsinki, Finland: Close to the Forest, Nature in the City. http://depts.washington.edu/open2100/resources/1_openSpaceSystems/open_Space_Systems/helsinki.pdf, Helsinki 2006

Organisation for Economic Cooperation and Development: Territorial Reviews, Helsinki, Finland, Paris 2003, p. 236

Vähä-Piikkiö, Inker/ Maijala, Olli (2005): "Helsinki" in Ann Caroll Werquin et al., Green Structure and Urban Planning, Luxembourg 2005, pp. 163–169

City of Helsinki: http://www.hel.fi/www/helsinki/en, 22.09.2014

Greater Helsinki Vision 2050 – International Ideas Competition, Jury Protocol, December 15, 2006 to May 31, 2007

Kotka

Antilla, Eija: Meripuisto pokkasi palkinnon, Kymen Sanomat, 13.09.2012, pp. 4–5

European Landscape Contractors Association: International ELCA Trend Award, Building with Green presented to the Finnish Project: Katariina Beach Park in the Port City of Kotka, http://www.szuz.cz/userfiles/file/trend_award_re-lease_2012.pdf, 22.09.2014

Flander, Jukka-Pekka: "The Finnish National Urban Park (NUP) Concept as Part of Sustainable Urban Planning," in Taina Veltheim/ Brita Pajari (Ed.), Forest Landscape Restoration in Central and Northern Europe, Joensuu 2005, pp. 139–144

Kosko, Juha: Huippupalkinto Meripuistolle, Kaupunkilehti Ankurri, 12.09.2012

Kotkan kaupunki: Welcome to Kotka! http://www4.kotka.fi/matkailulomakkeet/ kotka_english_web.pdf, Kotka 2008, p. 44

Kotkan kaupunki: Kotkan Kansallinen Kaupunkipuisto – Perustamisselvitys, Kotka: Kotkan kaupunki, http://www.visitkotka.fi/instancedata/prime_product_julkaisu/kotka/embeds/visitkotkawwwstructure/16993_ kkp_2013_web.pdf, Kotka 2013, p. 92

Leskinen, Pekka: Katariinan Meripuisto Kotkassa on Vuoden 2012 ympäristörakenne, Betoni-lehti, No. 3, 2012 http://www.betoni.com/Download/23785/bet1203_44-49.pdf, pp. 44–49

Ojansivu, Merja: MERI JA TUULI hallitsevat Katariinan Meripuistoa, Kunta Tekniikka, No. 1, 2013, http://lehti.kuntatekniikka.fi/sites/default/files/kt0113-PDf-WWW-hQ.pdf, pp. 6–11

Leverage from the EU (s.a.): The Empress's Park becomes the people's park, Leverage from the EU for Finnish environmental projects – European Union structural funds 2007-2013 (brochure), http://www.rakennerahastot.fi/rakennerahastot/tiedostot/esitteet/rakennerahasto_englanti.pdf, p. 3

We would like to thank the following people:

Ms. Elina Nummi (Project Manager for the Public Works Department, Streets and Parks Division of the City of Helsinki), Ms. Maria Jaakkola (Head of the Environmental Office, City Planning Department of the City of Helsinki), Mr. Heikki Laaksonen (Municipal Landscape Architect of the City of Kotka) and Mr. Seppo Närhi (Managing Director of the Landscape Contractors Association – Viheraluerakentajat ry).

France
Lille, Parc de la Deûle & Lyon Confluence

Berque, Augustin: Du geste à la cité. Formes urbaines et lien social au Japon, Paris 1993, p. 247

Berque, Augustin: Les raisons du paysage, Hazan, Paris 1995, p. 192

Blanc, Nathalie: "De l'écologie dans la ville," in Ethnologie française, Vol. 34 No. 4/2004, pp. 601–607

Bonnin, Philippe/ Clavel, Maïté: "Introduction. Quand la nature s'urbanise," in Ethnologie française, Vol. 40 No. 4/2010, pp. 581–587

Bourdin, Alain: "La ville se dit par evaluation," in: Cahiers internationaux de sociologie, Vol.1 No. 128–129/2010, pp. 117–134

Décamps, Henri: Ecologie: interfaces et ruptures, Séance solennelle de réception de nouveaux membres de l'Académie des sciences, élus le 16 décembre 2008 et le 24 février 2009

Bernard, Vincent/Deschodt, Laurent/Praud, Ivan et al: Archéoligie en nord – pas-de-Calais. Houplin-Ancoisne "Le marais de Santes" – Parc de la Deûle. Villeneuve-d'Ascq 2004

Dudzinski, Francis: La Deûle: renaissance d'une rivière, Lille, La Voix du Nord; Veurey, Le Dauphiné libéré, Coll. "Les patrimoines", Lille 2011, p. 51

Larrère, Catherine: Du bon usage de la nature, pour une philosophie de l'environnement, Paris 1997, p. 355

Louiset, Odette: "La Ville pour nature," in L'information géographique, Vol. 74 No. 3/2010, pp. 6–22

Lyon Confluence: Habiter à la confluence: un quartier actif, mixte et écologique, Lyon 2009, p. 15

Mollie, Caroline: Des arbres dans la ville, l'urbanisme végétal, Paris 2009, p. 254

Syndicat mixte du Parc de la Deûle: Le parc de la Deûle: des espaces pour découvrir, rêver et mieux vivre, Lille 1997, p. 45

Younès, Chris: Ville contre-nature, Paris 1999, p. 281

Netherlands
Breda, Borneo & Sporenburg

Adriaanse, Carlinde: On measuring and explaining neighbourhood success: a behavioural economic approach, Amsterdam 2011, p. 184

Aluvihare, Ruwan: A city in progress: physical planning in Amsterdam, Amsterdam 1994

Andela, Gerrie: Im Blickpunkt Niederlande: beispielhafte Ideen und Konzepte für Stadt und Landschaft, Munich 2002, p. 128

Hoeven, Casper van der/ Louwe, Jos: Amsterdam als stedelijk bouwwerk: een morfologische analyse, Amsterdam 2003, p.165

Hoog, Maurits de: 4x Amsterdam: ontwerpen aan de stad, Bussum 2005, p. 127

Hoog, Maurits de/ Vermeulen, Rick: Nieuwe ritmes van de stad: metropoolvorming in Amsterdam, Bussum 2009, p. 111

Koekebakker, Olof: Westergasfabriek culture park: transformation of a former industrial site in Amsterdam, Rotterdam 2003, p. 144

Masboungi, Ariella: Atelier Projet Urbain, Breda, faire la ville durable, Paris 2008, p. 143

Reijndorp, Arnold: Stadswijk: stedenbouw en dagelijks leven, Rotterdam 2004, p. 224

Schaap, Ton: Amsterdam, Rotterdam 2008, p. 80

United Kingdom
East London & Greenwich Millennium Village

Greater London Authority: East London Green Grid Supplementary Planning Guidance, London 2008, p. 65

Department for Communities and Local Government: Thames Gateway Parklands Vision, London 2008, p. 37

Meridian Delta Limited: Greenwich Millenium Village Design Code, London 2004, p. 216

iug
institut d'urbanisme
de grenoble

Authors
> Charles Ambrosino,
> Jennifer Buyck,
> Muriel Delabarre,
> Hendrika Kirchhoff,
> Mathieu Perrin,
> Melanie Schulte,
> Marcus Zepf.

Research Project
Institut d'Urbanisme de Grenoble
2012–2013

EUROPEAN
LANDSCAPE
ELCA CONTRACTORS
ASSOCIATION

MARCUS ZEPF (HG.)

Grün in der Stadt

Innovativ und nachhaltig planen
mit der urbanen Flora

jovis

Die Publikation ist das Ergebnis des Forschungsauftrages „Grün in der Stadt", der vom Institut d'urbanisme de Grenoble (IUG) im Auftrag der ELCA realisiert wurde.

Umschlagmotiv: Region Stuttgart, Shutterstock

Übersetzung ins Deutsche: Institut d'urbanisme de Grenoble (IUG)
Gestaltung: Institut d'urbanisme de Grenoble (IUG)
Satz: jovis Verlag: Yvonne Illig
Lithografie: Bild1Druck, Berlin
Druck und Bindung: Graspo CZ, a. s., Zlín

Bibliografische Information der Deutschen Nationalbibliothek
Die Deutsche Nationalbibliothek verzeichnet diese Publikation in der Deutschen Nationalbibliografie; detaillierte bibliografische Daten sind im Internet über http://dnb.d-nb.de abrufbar.

jovis Verlag GmbH
Kurfürstenstraße 15/16
10785 Berlin

www.jovis.de

jovis-Bücher sind weltweit im ausgewählten Buchhandel erhältlich. Informationen zu unserem internationalen Vertrieb erhalten Sie von Ihrem Buchhändler oder unter www.jovis.de.

ISBN 978-3-86859-362-4

Grün
in der Stadt

Strategie zu mehr Grün in Städten

Emmanuel Mony, Präsident der ELCA

Es ist wichtig, dass Grün und Natur stärker in das Blickfeld der europäischen Politik rücken. Das Bewusstsein von Bürgern und Entscheidungsträgern in Bezug auf den wirtschaftlichen und gesellschaftlichen Wert von urbanem Grün muss weiter geschärft werden: von historischen Gartenanlagen und privaten Gärten über Parkflächen und botanische Gärten bis zum Straßenbegleitgrün.

Die ELCA versteht sich dabei als Motor der Initiative «Die Grüne Stadt», die als gemeinsame Idee von deutschen und niederländischen Organisationen gegründet wurde mit dem Ziel, öffentliches Grün in der Stadt zu sichern und auszubauen. Neben Deutschland und Holland wird «Die Grüne Stadt» derzeit auch in der Schweiz, Frankreich, Spanien und Irland mit Erfolg umgesetzt.

Die ELCA ist davon überzeugt, dass die Thematik große Bedeutung hat, da die Grundfragen in nahezu allen Städten identisch sind: welche positiven städtebaulichen, sozialen und ökologischen Effekte gehen von Grün aus, wie gelingt die Finanzierung und Pflege von Grünflächen in Städten, welche Pflanzen und Pflanzsysteme bieten den größten Nutzen, welche positiven Effekte haben Pflanzen und speziell Bäume bei der Reduzierung von Feinstäuben?

Wir wollen zum Ausdruck bringen, dass der ökonomische Wert von Grün für unsere Gesellschaft viel höher liegt als allgemein angenommen. Weitere Informationen zu den deutschsprachigen Aktivitäten zur «Grünen Stadt» sind im Internet erhältlich unter www.die-gruene-stadt.de.

Der ELCA geht es um ein optimales Verhältnis von Verkehr, Kultur, Tourismus, Wirtschaft und städtischem Grün. Denn nur das richtige Grün am richtigen Ort kann eine positive und nachhaltige Wirkung entfalten. Daher sind wir auch gerne bereit, unsere Erfahrungen mit in neue Projekte einzubringen. Wir bieten daher unsere Mitarbeit, Zusammenarbeit und Unterstützung an. Wir wünschen Ihnen viel Glück und Erfolg bei der Umsetzung Ihrer richtig gesetzten Ziele!

Die European Landscape Contractors Association, ELCA, vertritt 16 nationale Berufsverbände aus Europa. Rund 50.000 Betriebe des Garten-, Landschafts- und Sportplatzbaus bieten 330.000 Menschen in ganz Europa Arbeitsplätze. Die Hauptaufgabe der mittelständisch geprägten Unternehmen sind Bau und Pflege von Hausgärten, Dachbegrünungen, Freiflächen im Wohnungsbau sowie Neuanlagen und Pflegearbeiten von öffentlichen Parks, Sportflächen und alle Arten von Grünanlagen.

Grün in der Stadt
Stadt am Wasser

Die Natur ist ohne Zweifel ein wichtiger Aspekt der heutigen Stadt. Urbane Grünflächen befriedigen vielfältige soziale Bedürfnisse und entsprechen dem zunehmenden ökologischen Bewusstsein der Stadtgesellschaft. Dieses Buch beleuchtet wichtige Trends der gegenwärtigen Planungspraxis und zeigt an innovativen Beispielen aus fünf europäischen Ländern, wie urbane Naturräume entworfen bzw. aufgewertet und in den städtischen Kontext integriert werden können. Alle ausgewählten Regionen und Projekte weisen zudem einen bestimmten Bezug zum Wasser auf, der selbst Ausdruck der Veränderungen in der Beziehung zwischen der Stadt und ihrer Umwelt ist. Schließlich werden in jedem der fünf nationalen Kontexte Projekte auf zwei verschiedenen geografischen Ebenen – derjenigen des gesamten Stadtgebiets und derjenigen des betreffenden Viertels –, in denen sich jeweils besondere Dynamiken zeigen, analysiert. Diese Vorgehensweise erlaubt es, die komplexen Zusammenhänge der Natur im städtischen Kontext besser zu begreifen.

Auf der Ebene des Stadtgebiets werden folgende Projekte vorgestellt:
> der Landschaftspark Region Stuttgart (Deutschland),
> das «Grüne Finger»-Konzept der Stadt Helsinki (Finnland),
> das integrierte Wassermanagement der Stadt Breda (Niederlande),
> der Parc de la Deûle im Süden des Gemeindeverbandes Lille Métropole (Frankreich),
> das geplante grüne Netzwerk in Ost-London (Großbritannien).

Anhand dieser Fallbeispiele soll – unter anderem – analysiert werden, inwiefern Natur angesichts zunehmender Zersiedelung als eine Basis für den territorialen Zusammenhalt, als «Infrastruktur» für ein Netzwerk sanfter Mobilität und Biotopverbunde oder als Substrat einer «Slow City» angesehen werden kann.

Auf der Ebene des Stadtviertels fiel die Wahl auf folgende Projekte:

> die Wassergärten in Lyon – La Confluence (Frankreich),
> die Berücksichtigung der Natur auf den dichtbewohnten künstlichen Inseln Borneo und Sporenburg in Amsterdam (Niederlande),
> der Katariina Strandpark auf einem ehemaligen Ölhafengelände der Stadt Kotka (Finnland),
> die Behandlung der Umwelt und der Landschaft innerhalb der Naturräume im Rahmen der Revitalisierung des ehemaligen Industrieviertels am Ufer des Karl-Heine-Kanals in Leipzig (Deutschland),
> das Greenwich Millennium Village in London (Großbritannien).

Anhand der ausgewählten Fallbeispiele lassen sich neue sozialräumliche Entwicklungen und innovative Planungstrends aufzeigen, die den räumlichen Wechselwirkungen von lokalen und regionalen Grünflächen eine besondere Bedeutung geben. Kleine Grünanlagen sowie begleitendes Grün und Restflächen ergeben im gesamtstädtischen Maßstab ein potenzielles Netzwerk für ein ganzheitliches ökologisches Konzept. Urbanes Grün verbunden mit suburbanen Landwirtschafts- und Erholungsräumen hilft, die Grenzen zwischen Stadt und Land neu zu definieren. Grün in der Stadt ist ebenfalls ein Vektor für soziale Beziehungen der jüngeren und der älteren Generation und schafft Verantwortungsbewusstsein für das eigene Lebensumfeld.

Darüber hinaus verändert die Natur auch das Bild der Stadt kontinuierlich, ein Transformationspotenzial, das Raumplaner und politische Entscheidungsträger bereits erfasst haben. Diejenigen Projekte und Pläne, die einer Logik der grünen Stadt folgen, können auch dazu einladen, abgewertete urbane Umgebungen mit anderen Augen zu sehen und in einem größeren Zusammenhang erscheinen zu lassen. Dieser großräumliche Kontext gewinnt insbesondere im Zusammenhang mit dem steigenden Wettbewerb unter den Städten und Regionen an Bedeutung.

In diesem Buch soll daher auch auf die Symbolkraft dieser neuen städtischen Natur eingegangen werden, ohne dabei die konkreten Aspekte – etwa die wirtschaftliche Dimension – der untersuchten Stadt-Natur-Konstruktionen zu vernachlässigen.

Deutschland
Finnland
Frankreich
Niederlande
Vereinigtes
Königreich

Region Stuttgart
Landschaftspark

H. KIRCHHOFF & M. SCHULTE

Innovativer Ansatz des Projektes

Der Landschaftspark Region Stuttgart besteht aus den Land-schaftsparks Neckar, Rems, Limes und Albtrauf. Er wurde mit dem Zweck eingerichtet, den Lebensraum für Menschen, Flora und Fauna aufzuwerten sowie den Wirtschaftsstandort Stuttgart zu sichern. Die Region Stuttgart ist einer der am stärksten ver-dichteten Ballungsräume in Deutschland, daher ist es wichtig, neben der Siedlungs-, Infrastruktur- und Verkehrsflächenent-wicklung auch die Entwicklung von Frei- und Erholungsräumen zu beachten, da diese als weicher Standortfaktor wesentlich zur Attraktivität der Region beitragen. Der Landschaftspark soll dabei nicht die Nutzung der Landschaft einschränken, sondern eine land- und forstwirtschaftlich genutzte und vielfältig gestaltete Landschaft definieren, die Siedlung, Wirtschaft und technische Infrastruktur miteinbezieht.

Im Jahr 1994 wurde von der Landesregierung im Rahmen des Ge-setzes zur Stärkung der Zusammenarbeit in der Region Stuttgart der Verband Region Stuttgart als politisches Sprachrohr der Re-gion gegründet. Seine Mitglieder werden alle fünf Jahre von den Bürgern gewählt. Im Jahr 2005 wurde die Trägerschaftsaufgabe für den regionalen Landschaftspark auf den Verband Region Stuttgart übertragen. Dadurch kann dieser die Projekte der einzelnen Land-schaftsparks mitfinanzieren und bietet so den konzeptionellen Rahmen für die Masterpläne. Dabei wurde für die Umsetzung ein Konzept aus zwei Säulen entwickelt: Zum einen werden nach dem Bottom-up-Prinzip in Kooperation mit den Kommunen, Fachbe-hörden und anderen Akteuren die Teilraumkonzepte entwickelt. Die zweite Säule besteht aus der Kofinanzierung des Verbands Region Stuttgart für die Umsetzung der ausgewählten Projekte. Das Konzept des Landschaftsparks Region Stuttgart hängt von der finanziellen Situation der Kommunen ab und besteht so lange, wie der politische Wille vorhanden ist.

Das Leitbild des Landschaftsparks Region Stuttgart lautet: «Landschaft nicht nur schützen, sondern auch aufwerten und gestalten». Das bedeutet, dass die Landschaft auch für Naher-holung und Tourismus nutzbar gemacht werden soll, etwa durch den Neubau von Fahrradwegen. Die einzelnen Teilparks Neckar, Rems, Limes und Albtrauf werden durch den Landschaftspark Region Stuttgart miteinander vernetzt, damit sind die Parks in das Konzept des regionalen Landschaftsparks eingebunden.

Akteurszusammenhänge

An der Gestaltung des Landschaftsparks Region Stuttgart sind der Verband Region Stuttgart, die Kommunen, Verbände und Bürger beteiligt. Durch den Bottom-up-Ansatz wird die Kooperation und Mitarbeit der verschiedenen Akteure sichergestellt. Ohne diese Kooperation ist die Umsetzung des Landschaftsparks Region Stuttgart nicht gewährleistet.

Wie die Zusammenarbeit funktioniert, wird vor allem bei der Erstellung der einzelnen Masterpläne deutlich: Im Rahmen von Workshops entwickeln die Kommunen sowie andere Beteiligte Ideen und Projekte, die ebenso in die Masterpläne einfließen wie Landschaftsanalysen, die die Stärken und Schwächen sowie die Besonderheiten der jeweiligen Region detailliert herausarbeiten. Die einzelnen Masterpläne sind bei veränderten Ansprüchen fortschreibungsfähig, da ihre Umsetzung für einen großen Zeitraum angesetzt ist. Für die einzelnen Landschaftsparks werden Leitbilder herausgearbeitet, an denen sich die einzelnen Projekte orientieren.

Der Landschaftspark ist ein informelles Instrument im Standortwettbewerb zwischen den Regionen. Das bedeutet, dass seine Anwendung nicht gesetzlich festgelegt ist und daher flexibel und frei ablaufen kann. Der Landschaftspark soll die bestehenden formellen Instrumente zur Sicherung sowie zum Schutz der Freiräume durch Mittel zur aktiven Gestaltung, Inszenierung und Inwertsetzung der Landschaft ergänzen. So soll die Entwicklung einer «grünen Infrastruktur» der Entwicklung der «grauen Infrastruktur» gegenübergestellt werden.

Finanzierungsrahmen

Der Verband Region Stuttgart finanziert im Rahmen einer Umlage die Projekte, die in den Masterplänen festgehalten werden. Dabei zahlen die Mitgliedskommunen einen Beitrag je nach Steuerkraft und Einwohneranzahl und beteiligen sich so an der Finanzierung der Projekte. Der maximale Beitrag liegt bei 50 Prozent. Die Kofinanzierung für verschiedene Projekte wird durch Wettbewerbe bestimmt, für die sich die Kommunen mit ihren Ideen bewerben können. Dabei sind die Qualität und die Einordnung in das Leitbild des regionalen Landschaftsparks ausschlaggebende Kriterien. Die Siegerprojekte werden von einer Jury aus dem politischen Gremium der Region ausgewählt. Das informelle Verfahren des Wettbewerbs wird verwendet, da es flexibel und unbürokratisch abläuft. Bei der Ver-

gabe ist die Jury frei in ihren Entscheidungen. Außerdem können sich auch Kommunen beteiligen, für die kein Masterplan vorliegt. Das Verfahren wird von den Kommunen positiv angenommen.

Der Verband Region Stuttgart übernimmt nach der Umsetzung der Projekte keine Verantwortung für die weitere Pflege und Instandhaltung. Dadurch wird verhindert, dass weitere Mittel für das Projekt angefordert werden und neue Investitionen für den Verband entstehen. Die Kommunen verpflichten sich somit im Rahmen der Kofinanzierung, für mindestens 15 Jahre die Pflege und Instandhaltung der Projekte zu übernehmen, um eine dauerhafte Verbesserung der Region zu gewährleisten.

Eine weitere Förderung der Projekte, neben der Kofinanzierung, geschieht durch die INTERREG-Programme. Dadurch können externe Mittel generiert und Teilprojekte umgesetzt werden.

Konsequenzen für die lokale Ökonomie sind nur marginal. Die geförderten Projekte sind in der Regel kleine Projekte, die daher auch nur kleine Verbesserungen hervorrufen.

Besonderheiten

Der Landschaftspark Region Stuttgart weist Besonderheiten auf: insbesondere die Kooperation mit und die Beteiligung von verschiedenen Akteuren schon bei der Erstellung der Masterpläne, die bisher nicht üblich war. Dadurch wird sichergestellt, dass die Interessen aller Akteure und ansässigen Gemeinden berücksichtigt werden. Diese Einbeziehung stärkt eine gemeinsame Identität der Region Stuttgart und motiviert die Kommunen auch nach der Fertigstellung der Projekte, das Ergebnis instandzuhalten. So wird eine nachhaltige Verbesserung der Region angestrebt.

Dadurch, dass ein freier Wettbewerb und kein klassisches Förderkonzept verwendet wird, ist der Verband Region Stuttgart in seinen Entscheidungen ungebunden und kann flexibel auf Veränderungen reagieren.

Der Landschaftspark Region Stuttgart wird dazu beitragen, dass in der verdichteten Region Stuttgart eine «grüne Infrastruktur» entsteht, die einen Gegensatz zur «grauen Infrastruktur» bildet und die Region für Anwohner und Touristen attraktiv macht.

Leipzig
Quartier an der weißen Elster/am Karl-Heine-Kanal

H. KIRCHHOFF & M. SCHULTE

Innovativer Ansatz des Projektes

Die deutsche Wiedervereinigung im Jahr 1990 läutete für Leipzig einen Wandel ein. So wurden im Jahr 2000 mit dem Beschluss des Stadtentwicklungsplans Wohnungsbau und Stadterneuerung (STEP W+S) wichtige Weichen für die Entwicklung von innerstädtischen Wohnquartieren gestellt. Als Konsequenz ist im Jahr 2005 der Konzeptionelle Stadt-teilplan Leipziger Westen (KSP West) beschlossen worden, der für den gründerzeitlichen Stadtteil Plagwitz vertiefende Aussagen und Maßnahmenpakete vorsieht. Neue Leitziele sollen eine strategische und nachhaltige städtebauliche Entwicklung bis zum Jahr 2020 ermöglichen, die Attraktivität und Lebensqualität in Plagwitz nachhaltig fördern und verbessern helfen.

Die Strategie rückt die identitätsstiftenden und quartiersbildprägenden baulichen Strukturen wie Denkmäler, Gewässer, Gleistrassen in Plagwitz in den Mittelpunkt. Damit konzentriert sich die Quartiersentwicklung auf Schwerpunkte. Im Rahmen der Bedeutung von Grün in der Stadt gelten die Erschließung des Gewässergrüns, die Entwicklung von Grünzonen auf bisherigen Gleistrassen sowie die sukzessive Sanierung des Straßenraumes als Aufwertungsmaßnahmen des öffentlichen Raums. Besonderers Augenmerk liegt auf dem Aspekt «grüne Räume schaffen und vernetzen» (vgl. Leipzig 2005, S. 16 f.). Parallel zum Auenwald im Osten soll im Westen auf dem ehemaligen Gebiet des Güterbahnhofs Plagwitz durch den «GleisGrünZug» ein weiteres grünes Band in Nord-Süd-Richtung entstehen. Freiraumbänder in Ost-West-Richtung, wie zum Beispiel der Stadtteilpark Plagwitz, der im Kontext der Weltausstellung EXPO 2000 als Fläche für Freizeit und Erholung auf einem ehemaligen Verladebahnhof, direkt am Karl-Heine-Kanal gelegen, umgesetzt wurde, verbinden die beiden großen Grünflächen miteinander.

Der Karl-Heine-Kanal und die Weiße Elster bilden im Stadtteil Plagwitz quartiersstrukturierende Elemente. Hohe Investitionssummen wurden für die Sanierung und Verlängerung des Karl-Heine-Kanals in Richtung Lindenauer Hafen bereitgestellt. In den letzten Jahren sind insbesondere die

Uferbereiche neugestaltet und historische Brückenverbindungen wieder instandgesetzt worden. In diesem Zusammenhang wurde auch ein Radwegenetz entlang des Kanals geschaffen. Neu angelegte kleine Kanaldurchstiche steigern die Attraktivität der bereits bestehenden Gewässerlandschaft und verbessern das Angebot an Freizeitmöglichkeiten für die Bewohner des Stadtteils Plagwitz. Durch den geplanten Gewässerverbund entsteht ein neues Naherholungsgebiet direkt in der Stadt. Die Möglichkeit, per Boot bald direkt vom Lindenauer Hafen über den Karl-Heine-Kanal in das Stadtzentrum und in die im Südraum neu entstehende Leipziger Seenlandschaft zu gelangen, soll zu einer Vernetzung und Verbesserung der Grün- und Gewässersysteme in der Stadt Leipzig beitragen (vgl. Stadt Leipzig 2006). Durch die angestrebte Verlängerung des Karl-Heine-Kanals in Richtung Lindenauer Hafen soll der Stadtteil Plagwitz einen weiteren Entwicklungsschub erhalten.

Mit der beginnenden Förderung im Rahmen des europäischen Fonds für regionale Entwicklung (EFRE 2007-2013) wurde der KSP West 2009 fortgeschrieben.

Akteurszusammenhänge

Hauptsächlich verantwortlich für die Konzipierung des Stadtteilplans und die weitere Entwicklung des Quartiers ist eine Projektgruppe der Stadtverwaltung. Diese wurde im Laufe des Prozesses von externen Fachleuten beraten. Des Weiteren bietet das Forum Leipziger Westen eine Plattform zum Austausch von Interessenslagen zwischen den verschiedenen Akteuren. Unternehmen, Bürger und Vereine können sich mit ihren Ideen einbringen und die weitere Quartiersentwicklung gemeinsam gestalten. Eine spezielle Plattform für die Weiterentwicklung von innerstädtischen Grünflächen bietet der Verein Nachbarschaftsgärten e. V., der Zwischennutzungen auf ehemaligen Brachflächen in Form von Urban Gardening zum Ziel hat (vgl. Website Forum Leipziger Westen).

Das Instrument des konzeptionellen Stadtentwicklungsplans beinhaltet ein Leitbild der künftigen Entwicklung, einen Transformationsplan, der den potenziellen Stadtumbau bis 2020 darstellt, und einen Aktionsfelderplan, der konkrete Maßnahmen für die Umsetzung benennt. Im Gegensatz zu städtebaulichen Rahmenplänen wird bewusst auf detaillierte, parzellenscharfe Vorgaben verzichtet.

Finanzierungsrahmen

Aufgrund der zunehmend knappen Haushaltslage der Stadt Leipzig setzte man bewusst auf eine Kombination diverser Förderinstrumente. Zum einen wurden traditionelle Instrumente der Städte-

bauförderung (Städtebauliche Erneuerung in Sanierungsgebieten und Stadtumbau Ost) eingesetzt: Derzeit befinden sich im Leipziger Westen sechs Sanierungsgebiete mit unterschiedlichen Schwerpunkten. Die Sanierung des Karl-Heine-Kanals und die Errichtung eines begleitenden Fuß- und Radwegs kosteten ca. 5,5 Millionen Euro. Weitere Investitionen der öffentlichen Hand beziehen sich auf Neubau und Sanierung von kanalquerenden

Ziegelbogenbrücken (7,8 Millionen Euro) und die Umnutzung ehemaliger Gleisanlagen zugunsten von Fuß- und Radwegen («Grüne Finger»: 1,1 Millionen Euro). Zum anderen ist vor allem das EU-Förderprogramm URBAN II für die Entwicklung des Leipziger Westens von großer Bedeutung. Im Zeitraum 2001-2008 stand ein Fördervolumen von ca. 14,5 Millionen Euro zur Verfügung. Hierbei wurde gezielt auf die Entwicklung und Verbesse-

rung stadträumlicher Qualitäten geachtet, ebenso wie auf die Entwicklung der lokalen Wirtschaftsstruktur sowie die Stärkung sozialer Qualitäten (vgl. Leipzig 2005, S. 43 ff.). Seit 2009 wird der Stadtteil Plagwitz im Rahmen des Förderprogramms EFRE 2007-2013 unterstützt. Der Schwerpunkt der Förderung liegt auf einer nachhaltigen Stadtentwicklung und der Revitalisierung von Brachflächen, wie zum Beispiel der Entwicklung des Lindenauer

Hafens als «attraktives urbanes Stadtquartier» am Wasser (http://www.leipzig.de/bauen-und-wohnen /stadtentwicklung/projekte/lindenauer-hafen/ Website der Stadt Leipzig).

Die städtisch geförderten Projekte dienten als Entwicklungsimpulse für private Investoren, die auch weiterhin mit eigenen Projekten zu einer steigenden Lebensqualität im Quartier zwischen dem Karl-Heine-Kanal und der Weißen Elster bei- tragen. Als Auswirkungen auf die Quartiersstruk- tur lassen sich die steigende Bevölkerungszahl, die Zunahme an tertiären Dienstleistungen und die verstärkte kulturelle Aktivität im Quartier – na- mentlich die Ansiedelung von Galerien, Künstlern und innovativen Firmen – benennen.

Besonderheiten

Der Leipziger Westen ist besonders durch die postsozialistischen urbanen Transformationspro- zesse gekennzeichnet, die sich nach der Wieder- vereinigung in ostdeutschen Städten abzeichne- ten. In Leipzig-Plagwitz manifestiert sich dieser Wandel in der Transformation eines ehemaligen Industrie- und Arbeiterviertels zu einem Stadtteil am Wasser mit besonderen Lebensqualitäten. Aufbauend auf den weichen Standortfaktoren Karl-Heine-Kanal und Weiße Elster konnte eine nachhaltige städtebauliche Entwicklung realisiert werden. Der Prozess der Revitalisierung ist aller- dings noch nicht vollständig abgeschlossen. Die Stadt Leipzig verfolgt weiterhin die Strategie, durch einen gezielten Ausbau von Gewässerstrukturen die stadträumlichen Qualitäten innerhalb des Quar-

tiers zu verbessern. Zusammen mit einer fokussierten Entwicklung von Grün- und Freiflächen auf Bereichen von bisherigen Gleistrassen und ehemaligen Industrieflächen erfolgt eine Aufwertung des öffentlichen Raums. Brachflächen werden gezielt weiterentwickelt, um so Trading-down-Effekten innerhalb des Quartiers gezielt entgegenzusteuern. In diesem Zusammenhang entstanden diverse grüne Wegenetze und Stadtteilparks entlang von sanierten Wasserwegen.

Aufbauend auf den genannten Umstrukturierungsprozessen konnte in den letzten Jahren insbesondere das Freizeit- und Kulturangebot stetig verbessert werden. Entlang des Karl-Heine-Kanals und der Weißen Elster entstanden gastronomische Einrichtungen, ein Kanu- und Ruderbootverleih sowie das Jugendzentrum Kanal 28. Eine wassertouristische

Inwertsetzung des Kanals wird durch das Passagierschiff MS Weltfrieden sowie durch das jährlich stattfindende Wasserfest zusätzlich gefördert. Der Karl-Heine-Kanal konnte durch die Sanierung und durch den Ausbau von Fuß- und Radwegen als Erlebnisraum wahrgenommen werden.

Das Quartier am Karl-Heine-Kanal und an der Weißen Elster gehört mittlerweile zu den begehrtesten Wohn- und Arbeitsstandorten in Leipzig. Die Nachhaltigkeit des Konzepts lässt sich anhand von hohen privaten Investitionen in den Wohnungsbestand und der damit verbundenen Reduzierung von Leerständen ermitteln. Ebenso verweisen steigende Einwohnerzahlen und die zunehmende Nachfrage nach Freizeitangeboten auf erwartbaren Erfolg.

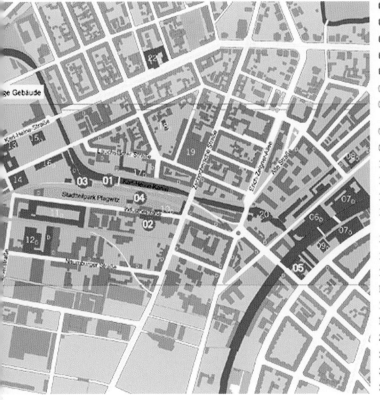

01_Stabbogenbrücke

02_Stadthäuser Industriestraße

03_Stelzenhaus[D]

04_Stadtteilpark Plagwitz mit altem Verlade

05_Stadthäuser >> Sweetwater >> Holbeins

06_Buntgarnwerke & Loftwohnungen >> Els

07_Buntgarnwerke // Handel, Dienstleistung Gewerbe, Loftwohnungen[D]

08_Museum für Druckkunst[D]

09_ehemaliges Heizhaus[D]

10_Stadthausprojekt >> Wagnersche Häuse

11_Konsumzentrale[D] Architekt: Fritz Höger

12_Städtischer Gewerbehof[D]

13_Technologie- und Gewerbepark Plagwitz Business-Innovation-Center

14_Parkhaus

15_GaraGe // Jugendtechnologiezentrum[D]

16_Gewerbezentrum Weißenfelser Straße[D]

17_Feuerwache[D]

18_Mütterzentrum[D]

19_Einkaufszentrum >> Elsterpassage

20_Studiogebäude >> MDR Riverboat

21_Baumwollspinnerei[D]

22_Schaubühne Lindenfels[D]

23_Kanal 28[D]

Deutschland
Finnland
Frankreich
Niederlande
Vereinigtes
Königreich

Helsinki
«Masterplan 2002», «Greater Helsinki Vision 2050» & «Grüne Finger»

MATHIEU PERRIN

Innovativer Ansatz des Projektes

Im Jahr 2002 wies das 187 Quadratkilometer große Stadtgebiet von Helsinki 5654 Hektar öffentliche Grünflächen auf. Auf
1000 Einwohner kommen damit 4,2 Hektar Grünfläche. Davon
sind 63 Prozent Stadtwald, 17 Prozent Parklandschaft und elf
Prozent Felder und Wiesen. Im Rahmen des Masterplans 2002,
welcher 2003 verabschiedet wurde und seit 2006 in Kraft ge-
treten ist, hat die Stadt Helsinki ein Netz von Grünräumen vorgeschlagen: Natürliche Räume, Parks und Grünanlagen sollen
kombiniert werden, sodass Vernetzungen und Spaziergänge
zwischen den verschiedenen Grünräumen möglich sind. Das Ensemble organisiert sich um große Naturachsen und die «Grünen
Finger», welche von der Küste aus die Stadt durchqueren und bis
ins Hinterland reichen (siehe «Masterplan 2002» und seine Netz-
struktur aus «Grünen Fingern»). Das Stadtplanungsamt der Stadt
Helsinki hat die Abgrenzung und Eintragung der landschaftsbe-
zogenen Flächen nach funktionellen, visuellen und ökologischen
Kriterien festgelegt. Sie sind vor allem wieder an die zentralen Elemente der natürlichen Geographie – Fluss- und Küstengebiete –
angeschlossen worden.

Im Jahre 2006 haben der finnische Umweltminister sowie
14 Städte und Gemeinden der Region Helsinki den internationalen Wettbewerb «Greater Helsinki Vision 2050» durchgeführt.
Dabei sollten strategische und innovative Ideen sowie Trends für
das Metropolgebiet, welches sich über ca. 3000 Quadratkilometer erstreckt, gesammelt werden. Die Jury, welche aus Politikern, lokalen Experten und Hochschullehrern bestand, hat am
Ende des Jahres 2007 die Vorschläge prämiert, die als passend
für die zukünftige Entwicklung von Helsinki befunden wurden.
Auch wenn die natürliche Dimension nicht zwangsläufig das
zentrale Thema im Wettbewerb war, sollte sie sich doch als wichtiges Kriterium bei der Bewertung erweisen.

Als Gewinner ging aus diesem Wettbewerb das Projekt Emerald
hervor, welches von der Agentur WSP Finland und dem Architekten

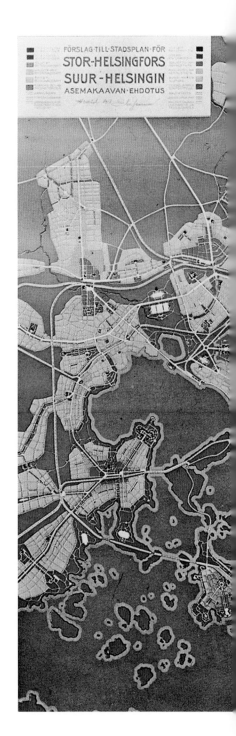

Juha Eskolin erarbeitet wurde. Die Architekten haben die Jury auch dadurch überzeugt, dass sie die Naturräume vorausschauend für die Stadtregion Helsinki berücksichtigt haben. Das Konzept greift die Idee eines Netzes von Naturräumen auf, die sich um die «Grünen Finger» zwischen Küste und Hinterland manifestieren. Im Gebiet um die Naturachsen setzt sich in einem ganz anderen Maßstab das gleiche Muster fort und bildet eine neue ganzheitliche Struktur, die auf der Ebene der Stadtregion wahrgenommen werden kann.

Funktionen und Rolle des Grüns in der Stadt

Im Stadtgebiet Helsinki sind die Naturflächen vor allem Erholungsräume. Noch bevor die ökologische Frage in den 70er Jahren das Thema «Grün» ins Bewusstsein der Öffentlichkeit brachte, nutzte die lokale Bevölkerung diese Räume schon stark für Freizeitaktivitäten. Daher hat sie eine gewisse Verbundenheit mit diesen Orten. Außerdem haben die Stadtbehörden durch das Muster «Grüne Finger», das auch das urbane Gefüge mitstrukturiert, einen Zugang zu den Naturflächen für möglichst viele Einwohner geschaffen. Die «Grünen Finger» sollen für alle Bürger über Promenaden und Wege in weniger als 15 Minuten zu Fuß erreichbar sein. Im Übrigen ist es eines der Ziele des engmaschigen Netzes, welches sich um die «Grünen Finger» figuriert, die «sanfte Mobilität» zu fördern.

Die in den Masterplan 2002 eingegangenen Analysen haben sich ausgiebig mit dem Natur- und dem Kulturerbe beschäftigt und die große Bedeutung erwiesen, die der Schutz bestimmter Bereiche von ökologischem Interesse sowie öffentlicher Gärten und Parks aus dem 19. Jahrhundert für die Stadt und ihre Bewohner hat.

Im Maßstab der Region Helsinki haben die Autoren des Projekts Emerald geplant, die bebauten Gebiete durch einen aufwertenden Grüngürtel einzurahmen, um der Zersiedlung entgegenzuwirken. Für die Konzeptentwickler ist das Wachsen der stadt- und damit verbrauchernahen Landwirtschaft auch ein Mittel, die Qualität der Grünflächen abzusichern. Damit unterscheidet sich dieser Vorschlag für das Metropolgebiet im Rahmen des Wettbewerbs «Greater Helsinki Vision 2050» von den Leitlinien des Masterplans 2002, da in dem letztgenannten Dokument die landwirtschaftliche Thematik nicht vorrangig ist. Vermutlich sind der größere Maßstab und der langfristige Horizont des Wettbewerbs eine Erklärung für den Kontrast. Als wichtigster Punkt wird die Grünstruktur als ein strategisches Gestaltungselement für die Stadtregion Helsinki im lokal- und geopolitischen Sinn vorgeschlagen. Es sind die Naturräume, die das Bindeglied für eine gemeinsame Vision bilden. So lassen sich mithilfe der unterschiedlichen Akteure der Metropolregion endlich die mannigfaltigen Schwierigkeiten überwinden, die einem solchen Projekt bislang entgegenstanden.

Die Idee einer Grünstruktur hat, wenn auch auf mehr zufällige Art, in der Geschichte der Planung Helsinkis lange Spuren hinterlassen. Bereits 1918 veröffentlichten die Architekten Eliel Saarinen, Einar Sjöström und Bertel Jung – dieser war damals als Planer bei der Stadt angestellt – einen ersten Plan zur Erweiterung für ein Gebiet, das sich später zur Stadtregion Helsinki entwickelte (Pro Helsingfors). Dieses Planungsdokument, das mit privaten Mitteln finanziert wurde, war neu für die Epoche und schlug bereits eine Einbettung der Parks und der landwirtschaftlichen Flächen, die die bebauten Zonen der Stadt räumlich voneinander trennten, in die Stadtstruktur vor. Obwohl der Plan nicht umgesetzt wurde, haben später viele der hier vorgebrachten Ideen die lokale räumliche Organisation beeinflusst. Nach den 70er Jahren wurden erstmalig Planungsdokumente verabschiedet, die das gesamte Gemeindegebiet (ohne Seeflächen) abdeckten. So hat sich allmählich eine grüne radiale Struktur entwickelt, die von der Küste über die Stadt bis in das Hinterland reicht – die «Grünen Finger» aus Parks, Wäldern, Wiesen und Feldern.

Der Masterplan 2002 brach nicht mit dem Bestehenden, sondern versuchte im Gegenteil, die historische Dimension und die räumliche Realität zu integrieren. Bemerkenswert ist, wenn auch in einem anderen Maßstab, bis zu welchem Punkt das Projekt Emerald historische räumliche Konzepte in einer vorausschauenden Vorgehensweise wieder aufgegriffen hat.

Akteurszusammenhänge

Folgende Akteure sind an der Ausarbeitung und an der operationellen Umsetzung des Masterplans 2002 beteiligt:

- die Stadt Helsinki (sie besitzt ca. 70 Prozent der Flächen im Gemeindegebiet; die gewählten Vertreter der Stadt stimmen über den Masterplan ab),
- das Planungsreferat der Stadt Helsinki (Reflexion und Ausarbeitung der Pläne),
- das Amt für öffentliche Bauarbeiten mit seinen verschiedenen Abteilungen (Gestaltung, Bau, Renovierung, Instandhaltung von Grünflächen),
- das Amt für Umwelt der Stadt Helsinki (Schutz und Pflege von Naturräumen),

• die privaten Firmen, welche das Amt für öffentliche Bauarbeiten der Stadt Helsinki zur Realisierung und Pflege der Projekte beauftragt,
• Die Einwohner der Stadt Helsinki, die sich am
Programm des Masterplans beteiligen. Sie tragen durch ihre freiwillige Teilnahme und Unterstützung zur Erhaltung von Grünflächen in der
Stadt bei.

Im Rahmen des internationalen Wettbewerbs
«Greater Helsinki Vision 2050» sind die folgenden
Akteure beteiligt:
• 14 Städte und Gemeinden der Agglomeration
Helsinki (Helsinki, Espoo, Vantaa Kauniainen,
Kerava, Tuusula, Järvenpää, Nurmijärvi, Mänt-
sälä, Pornainen, Hyvinkää, Kirkkonummi, Vihti
und Sipoo) sowie das finnische Umweltministe-

rium, das für die Eröffnung und die Finanzie-
rung des Wettbewerbs verantwortlich ist,
• die Jury, die sich aus Vertretern von Politik und
Wissenschaft sowie anderen Fachleuten zu-
sammensetzt,
• 86 Wettbewerbsteilnehmer, darunter auch das
Gewinnerteam des Projekts Emerald: das Büro
WSP Finland mit den Architekten Juha Eskolin,
Jenni Lautso, Ilona Mansikka und Tuomas
Vuorinen.

Die Stadt Helsinki verabschiedete neben dem
Masterplan 2002 das «Green Area Programme» für
den Zeitraum von 1999 bis 2008. Wesentlicher In-
halt dieses Programms ist unter anderem ein Plan,
in dem die Gemeinden Gebiete ausweisen, die
dem Schutz und Erhalt von Grün- und Freiflächen

dienen. Die in diesem Dokument erarbeiteten Richtlinien sind im Masterplan 2002 berücksichtigt. Die Stadt Helsinki zeichnet ihre Vorgehensweise aus, städtebauliche und freiraumplanerische Wettbewerbe auf internationaler Ebene auszuloben. So initiierte sie im Jahr 2011 einen Wettbewerb, in dem Strategien für die zukünftige Entwicklung des innenstadtnahen Gebiets Eteläsatama entwickelt werden sollten. Im Jahr 2012 wurde ein Wettbewerb ausgelobt, der ein modernes Belichtungskonzept für das Stadtquartier Kruunuvuorenranta zum Ziel hatte.

öffentliche Arbeiten bevorzugt behandelt werden. Das Amt beurteilt die diversen Grün- und Freiflächen nach dem Bedarf an Pflege. Es initiierte 2005 das Programm «Good Things Grown in Helsinki», das die Bürger motivieren sollte, sich freiwillig an der Instandhaltung von öffentlichen Grünflächen zu beteiligen. Durch Unterstützung von privaten Unternehmen konnten zusätzliche Mittel gewonnen werden, die der Gestaltung des öffentlichen Raumes dienen.

Die im Masterplan 2002 festgehaltenen Grünstrukturen und Naturräume («Grüne Finger») zielen nicht auf die explizite Herstellung neuer Parkflächen ab, sondern vielmehr auf das Zusammenführen der verschiedenen vorhandenen Strukturen, um damit neue Landschaftsformen zu generieren. Hierbei geht es insbesondere darum, die verschiedenen Formen urbanen Grüns in das Bewusstein zu rücken. Der Masterplan enthält keine revolutionären konzeptionellen Vorstellungen: Vielmehr dient er als Orientierungsrahmen, der die vorhandenen Grünstrukturen stärken und bewahren hilft.

Die Vorstellung, das Netzwerk von Naturräumen («Grüne Finger») auf die metropolitane Ebene der Agglomeration Helsinki zu übertragen, birgt große Herausforderungen. So müssen neue Strategien entwickelt werden, um die zahlreichen Akteure zusammenzuführen. Die Naturräume sind allerdings im regionalen Kontext zu sehen und für den Ballungsraum Helsinki erscheint es sinnvoll, dies ebenfalls auf institutioneller Ebene festzuhalten. Im Gegensatz zur Verkehrsinfrastruktur werden die Investitionen in öffentliche Grünflächen von den Planern nicht direkt als Vorteil wahrgenommen. Diese Konzeption der Naturräume als raumordnendes Element für das Bild der Metropole Helsinki kann als innovativer Ansatz angesehen werden, der dazu beiträgt, Stadt und Natur als ein vernetztes System zu begreifen.

Freiraumplanerische Aktivitäten organisieren und gliedern Räume. Sie sind von großer Bedeutung als Strukturelemente, die aus institutionellen und politischen Entscheidungen hervorgehen. Durch die Vernetzung von bestehenden grünen Freiräumen und die Anlage neuer Parklandschaften kann der Zusammenhalt zwischen den einzelnen Gemeinden in der Agglomeration Helsinki gestärkt werden. Die Auslobung städtebaulicher und freiraumplanerischer Wettbewerbe ist ein wichtiges Instrument, um neue Ideen und Vorstellungen entstehen zu lassen. Die Stadt Helsinki folgt diesem Ansatz seit einigen Jahren und kann dadurch wesentliche Erfolge erzielen.

Finanzierungsrahmen

Der Stadtrat von Helsinki beschließt jährlich die Summen, die für die Herstellung und Pflege von Grünflächen in der Stadt ausgegeben werden, wobei bestimmte Projekte auf Empfehlung der Abteilung für Straßenbau und Grünflächen des Amts für

Kotka
Katariina Strandpark

MATHIEU PERRIN

Innovativer Ansatz des Projektes

Der Katariina Strandpark breitet sich über 20 Hektar an der Süd-spitze der zentralen Insel Kotkas aus. Die Einrichtung dieses Na-turraums stellt mit seinen ökologischen Qualitäten und Reizen für die Bevölkerung einen Wendepunkt in der Geschichte der Stadt Kotka dar. Die erste Besonderheit des Parks liegt in der industri-ellen Vergangenheit seiner Nutzung. In den 30er und 40er Jahren des 20. Jahrhunderts wurden in diesem Bereich gleichzeitig mit der Entwicklung des Ölhafens von Kotka mehrere Lagertanks für Kohlenwasserstoffe installiert. In den 50er und 60er Jahren, im Laufe derer der Komplex seine größte Aktivität erfuhr, wurde die Anlage vergrößert. Sie zählte bis zu 56 Lagertanks und umfasste eine Gesamtlagerkapazität von 400.000 Kubikmetern. Als sich die Hafenindustrie in einen anderen Bereich der Agglomeration verlagerte und die Pachtverträge mit den Ölgesellschaften im Jahr 2000 ausliefen, konnte die Stadt eine neue Nutzung für das Ge-lände ins Auge fassen.

Die auf dem Gelände ansässigen Betriebe waren vertraglich ver-pflichtet, die Böden zu sanieren. Zwischen 2003 und 2006 wur-den in diesem Rahmen 100.000 Tonnen Erde, die mit Kohlen-wasserstoffen, Lösungsmitteln oder Blei hoch kontaminiert waren, gesäubert. Im Herbst des Jahres 2004 präsentierten die Stadt-werke Kotka erste Entwürfe für die Einrichtung des Parks. Gleich im Anschluss an diese Skizze und parallel zu den Sanierungsmaß-nahmen begannen die Bauarbeiten. Seit Herbst 2006 ist der Park der Öffentlichkeit zugänglich, doch gleichzeitig gehen die Arbeiten weiter: Die Bodensanierung wird fortgesetzt und der Park soll um neue Anlagen und Einrichtungen erweitert werden.

Im Jahr 2012 hat der Katariina Strandpark zwei wichtige Aus-zeichnungen erhalten. Er wurde mit dem internationalen Trend-preis «Bauen mit Grün» der European Landscape Contractors Association (ELCA) prämiert. Die Jury hob unter anderem den vorbildlichen Charakter dieser Umwandlung einer belasteten In-dustriebrache in einen öffentlichen und grünen Erholungsraum hervor. Außerdem wurde der Park mit dem «Preis der umwelt-gerechten Gestaltung 2012» des Zentralverbands für finnischen Gartenbau (Puutarhaliitto ry) und des Verbands der finnischen Bauindustrie (Rakennusteollisuus RT ry) ausgezeichnet. Jedes Jahr prämiert das Komitee ein Projekt aufgrund seiner bemer-kenswerten ästhetischen, funktionellen und umweltfreundlichen Qualitäten. Der Park verfügt über einen hohen Freizeitwert.

Einer der besonderen Schwerpunkte liegt auf der Nutzungsvielfalt für die Besucher des Grüns. Manche Räume und Anlagen sind hauptsächlich Sport- und Spielaktivitäten gewidmet (eine großzügige Rasenfläche, ein Beachvolleyballplatz, ein Skatepark, Discgolf-Körbe, Kinderspielplätze und Outdoor-Fitnessgeräte etc.), andere Orte dienen eher der Geselligkeit (Picknick- und Grillplätze) oder können für Wanderungen und Meditation (Spazierwege durch reichhaltige Flora und Fauna, Aussichtspunkte und Sitzmöglichkeiten, ein Meditationslabyrinth, eine isolierte kleine Insel, auf welcher symbolträchtig ein Anker steht) genutzt werden. Der Park ist als ein generationenübergreifender Ort der Begegnung konzipiert. Außerdem stellt das Grün, das die Pflanzenräume, Steinformen und Wasserflächen verbindet, eine neue Beziehung zur Umwelt her. Das ökologische Anliegen, welches sich in den vielen Anstrengungen zur Förderung der Entwicklung artenreicher Lebensräume auf dieser ehemals belasteten Fläche erkennen lässt, markiert den Übergang von einer industrielleren in eine grünere Phase. Der Park bietet seinen Besuchern die Möglichkeit, dieses Gebiet

wiederzuentdecken. Es wurde unter anderem ein Aussichtsturm zur Beobachtung von Vögeln, die im benachbarten Erlenwald oder in den Feuchtgebieten des Parks nisten, installiert.

Das Grün hat auch einen positiven Einfluss auf das Image der Stadt. Die Südspitze der zentralen Insel Kotkas, die bislang mit der lokalen Ölhafenindustrie verbunden wurde, erscheint nun in neuem Licht – einem Licht, das auf die gesamte Agglomeration ausstrahlt, die zeitweise unter dem Verlust ihrer wirtschaftlichen Bedeutung gelitten hat. Als Symbol dieser Entwicklung wurde kürzlich die Restaurierung der Ruinen des Ende des 18. Jahrhunderts errichteten Katariina Fort beschlossen, die seit den 50er Jahren zwischen den Lagertanks für Kohlenwasserstoffe eingezwängt waren.

Der Niedergang des Ölhafens und seiner Industrie in den letzten Jahrzehnten des 20. Jahrhunderts bedeutete für mehrere finnische Seestädte ein beträchtliches Problem. Obwohl die Verlagerung dieser Aktivitäten in stadtfernere Gebiete gelegentlich interessante Flächen freisetzte, hielt sich oft das schlechte Image des ehemaligen Industriegebietes, das häufig auch die ganze Stadt betraf. Die

Erneuerung dieses Images wurde somit zur Herausforderung. In diesem Sinne nahmen mehrere Städte umfangreiche Stadtentwicklungsprojekte auf den ehemaligen Hafenstandorten in Angriff, wie zum Beispiel in Helsinki-Jätkäsaari, Helsinki-Kalasatama oder Oulu-Toppilansaari.

Ab Mitte der 80er Jahre begann in Kotka die Idee zu keimen, diese ehemalige Industrie- und Hafenstadt in eine Agglomeration von Parks und Gärten zu verwandeln. Mithilfe der Natur sollten das Bild der Stadt und die lokale Identität erneuert werden. Seitdem haben die Stadtwerke ein inkrementelles Verfahren eingeführt, mit dem das grüne Netz Kotkas schrittweise mit neuen Projekten, welche die bestehende Struktur komplettieren, ergänzt wird. Im Laufe der 90er Jahre wurde der Wassergarten Sapokka, der aus dieser grünen Politik entstanden ist, mehrmals ausgezeichnet. Dies hat der Stadt zu einer breiteren Bekanntheit in der Öffentlichkeit verholfen.

Akteurszusammenhänge

Die Verwirklichung des Katariina Strandparks ist vor allem dem Durchsetzungswillen der Stadt Kotka zu verdanken, die seit zwei Jahrzehnten eine ehrgeizige Politik zugunsten von Grün und Naturräumen vorantreibt. In diesem Zusammenhang muss auf die bedeutende Rolle des Landschaftsarchitekten Heikki Laaksonen hingewiesen werden, der seit 1985 mit seiner Schaffenskraft die Stadt Kotka umwandelt und auch die Gestaltung des Katariina Strandparks geleitet hat. Der verantwortliche Landschaftsgärtner war Tomi Uusitalo, der für die Gesellschaft Pihat Oy Uusitalo arbeitet. Die Savaterra Oy, eine Gesellschaft, die sich auf die Behandlung von belasteten Böden sowie Industrieabfällen und Stadtmüll spezialisiert hat, führte im Auftrag der Ölgesellschaften die Bodensanierung durch. Das südöstliche finnische Regionalzentrum für Umwelt (Kaakkois-Suomen Ympäristökeskus) hat die Stadt Kotka in diesem Grünprojekt begleitet.

Seit einiger Zeit hat die Stadt Kotka Schritte unternommen, um ihr Netz von Grünanlagen und Naturräumen vom finnischen Umweltministerium als nationalen Stadtpark (Kansallinen Kaupunkipuisto) anerkennen zu lassen. Dieser Status, der seit dem Inkrafttreten des Gesetzes über die Bodennutzung und den Bau im Jahr 2000 vorgesehen ist, lehnt

sich eng an den schwedischen Rahmen an: Es kann ein nationaler Stadtpark gegründet werden, um die Ästhetik der Kultur- und Naturlandschaft, die historischen Merkmale sowie die Qualitäten eines urbanen Bereichs im Hinblick auf Städtebau, Soziales und Freizeit zu schützen und zu bewahren. Zu diesem Zweck sollen die lokalen Behörden in Zusammenarbeit mit dem Regionalzentrum für Umwelt einen Bewirtschaftungsplan erarbeiten, der die gültigen Pflegebedingungen und Nutzungsmodalitäten für die betroffenen Flächen festlegt. Gebiete, die wichtige Naturräume für die Erhaltung einer Biodiversität im Stadtmilieu, freie oder bebaute Kulturbereiche von historischem Interesse für die Stadt oder das Land sowie Parks und Grün mit hohen ästhetischen Werten und Gestaltungsqualitäten umfassen, sollen als nationale Stadtparks anerkannt werden. Außerdem sollen diese Gebiete zur ökologischen Kontinuität beitragen, indem die Wechselwirkungen mit den Naturräumen am Stadtrand erleichtert werden. Die Stadt Kotka zählt auf ihr hochwertiges Netz von Grünflächen und

hat ca. 1,2 Millionen Euro in die Verwirklichung des Parks investiert. Die Europäische Union hat zum Projekt mit ihren Strukturfonds in Höhe von 121.000 Euro beigetragen.

Das Image der Stadt Kotka, das hauptsächlich durch ihre Industrie und ihren Ölhafen geprägt war, hat sich grundlegend verändert. Die lokalen Touristeninformationszentren werben vor allem mit der Qualität des Parks und der Gärten, besonders bei den russischen Besuchern, die aus Sankt Petersburg kommen. Die Unternehmer und Investoren entdecken die Stadt mit einem moderneren und dynamischeren Gesicht ebenfalls neu – Grünflächen oder Gebäude mit markanter Architektur haben die Industriebrachen, Symbol des schlechten wirtschaftlichen Klimas Ende der 80er Jahre, ersetzt.

Im Jahr 2012 hat die Stadt Kotka ungefähr drei Millionen Euro (0,8 Prozent des Gemeindebudgets) für ihr Grünflächenamt verwendet. Abgesehen davon, dass die Grünanlagen auch Annehmlichkeiten für die Einwohner bieten, kann die Summe hinsichtlich des Imagegewinns als eine relativ rentable Investition betrachtet werden.

Fazit

Es mag paradox klingen, einen Park auf dieser Ölindustriebrache einzurichten, unter anderem aufgrund hochkontaminierter Böden, welche die Umwandelung des Gebiets in einen Naturraum stark erschwerten. Im Übrigen standen die Gelände an der Südspitze der zentralen Insel Kotkas beim Hotelgewerbe hoch im Kurs. Aber vermutlich trägt gerade die Einstellung hinsichtlich solcher Herausforderungen zum Imagewandel und zur Veränderung der Mentalitäten bei. Der Erfolg der Stadt Kotka mit ihren Parks und Gärten kann so gesehen ein Beispiel für andere Agglomerationen sein, insbesondere für diejenigen, die mit dem Niedergang ihrer industriellen und umweltbelastenden Aktivitäten konfrontiert sind.

Mit nur wenig mehr als 50.000 Einwohnern ist Kotka heute aufgrund seiner Grünplanung sehr bekannt geworden. Hauptnutznießer dieser Politik sind, obwohl die Stadt auch für Touristen und Investoren eindeutig attraktiver geworden ist, vermutlich die Einwohner selbst, die am meisten unter dem wirtschaftlichen Niedergang und der damit einhergehenden Stigmatisierung gelitten haben. Die Grünprojekte können mit ihrem Potenzial, die Wahrnehmung der Umgebung zu verändern, als relevante Option betrachtet werden, um ein Gebiet und seinen Bürgern neue Impulse zu geben und Mitnahmeeffekte für die Wirtschaft und die Stadt zu erzeugen.

Parks, um diese Anerkennung zu erlangen, die die seit zwei Jahrzehnten umgesetzten Bemühungen würdigen würde. Das Parkprojekt kann auch als ein Mittel zur Bündelung von lokalen Kräften um diesen grünen und natürlichen Reichtum der Gegend herum angesehen werden.

Finanzierungsrahmen

Die Bodensanierungskosten von ungefähr zehn Millionen Euro wurden von den betroffenen Ölgesellschaften übernommen. Die Stadt Kotka

Deutschland
Finnland
Frankreich
Niederlande
Vereinigtes
Königreich

Lille Métropole
Parc de la Deûle

MURIEL DELABARRE

Innovativer Ansatz des Projektes

Der Park wurde auf einer 350 Hektar großen Fläche entlang des Kanals der Deûle, in den Zwischenräumen der Industriebrache und des Stadtrandgebiets von Lille, geplant. Bereits im Jahr 1960 wurde die Idee eines breiten Grünzugs zwischen der Stadt Lille und dem Kohlenbecken von Lens auf den Weg gebracht. Dieses Vorhaben wurde allerdings erst 1993 durchgeführt, als Stimmen zugunsten des Lebensumfelds, des Umweltschutzes sowie einer besseren Integration der Landwirtschaft laut wurden. Das Projekt wurde offiziell anlässlich der Feierlichkeiten zu «Lille 2004, Kulturhauptstadt Europas» übergeben. Heute ist dieses Gebiet von einem Netz von Grünräumen überzogen, das eine ökologische und landschaftliche Verbindung zwischen seinen verschiedenen Teilen sichert. 2006 wurde der Park mit dem französischen Landschaftspreis des Umweltministeriums und 2009 mit dem ersten «Landschaftspreis des Europarats» ausgezeichnet. Diese zwei Auszeichnungen haben vermutlich zum Bekanntheitsgrad des Projekts beigetragen. Der Parc de la Deûle wird derzeit als Prototyp einer neuen Strategie für die Ausarbeitung öffentlicher Räume auf Ebene der Stadtregion, welche die benachbarten Landwirtschaftsbetriebe und Naturgebiete integriert, betrachtet.

Der Park greift die kraftvollen Linien des Gewässernetzes, des Parzellenplans sowie der Reliefformen auf. Die Inszenierung dieser grünen Infrastruktur wurde entlang gut markierter Wanderwege erarbeitet, die drei unterschiedliche Landschaftsthemen eröffnen:

- die «wiedergefundene Natur», mit dem Ziel, zur Wiedereroberung der Industriebrachen, zur Wiederherstellung natürlicher Lebensräume sowie zur Aufwertung der bestehenden Feuchtgebiete und der unterschwelligen ökologischen Lagequalität beizutragen;
- die «gezähmte Natur», mit dem Ziel, die landwirtschaftlich geprägten Gegenden durch Wiesen-, Hecken- und Grabenwiederherstellungen aufzuwerten sowie eine breit gefächerte Landwirtschaft und ihre Produkte, auch die Erzeugung in ökologisch kontrolliertem Anbau, zu fördern;
- die «geträumte Natur», mit dem Ziel, eine grüne Ästhetik durch einen botanischen Ziergarten, der einen Lebensraum für Pflanzen und Tiere bildet, zu entwickeln.

Der Park bietet verschiedenartiges öffentliches Grün, zum Beispiel einen mehrere 100 Meter langen Boulevard (Grande Allée de Wavrin), der die Stadt Wavrin von nun an direkt mit den Ufern des Kanals der Deûle verbindet, sowie Promenaden, die Brachen, Wälder, Feuchtwiesen und Felder durchziehen. Andernorts stellt

der Garten Mosaïc, Kernstück des Parks, eine Reihe von Themenräumen aus, welche die landschaftlichen Traditionen der Agglomeration Lille betonen. Die landschaftliche Gesamtstruktur sichert die Kohärenz zwischen den vielfältigen öffentlichen Grünarten. Die Landschaftsarchitekten Jacques Simon und Yves Hubert, die als Bauleiter im Rahmen dieses Projekts ausgewählt wurden, haben den Kanal als einen Leitfaden betrachtet, um die verschiedenen Bestandteile des Parks zu verbinden. Sie haben außerdem die erste Achse mit einem zweiten, gewundenen Wasserlauf, der bisher eine Drainageanlage für die landwirtschaftlichen Wasser der Deûle-Ebene bildete, verdoppelt. Alle geplanten Teile des Parks sind dank mehr oder weniger strukturierender Bindungen miteinander vernetzt. Sie setzen die Räume, die in den Bereich der drei im Projekt identifizierten Naturformen («wiedergefundene», «gezähmte» und «geträumte») fallen, in Beziehung zueinander. Bei der Bearbeitung der inszenierten Natur wurden außerdem die landwirtschaftlichen und städtischen Flächen berücksichtigt. Auf der Grundlage einer partnerschaftlichen Vorgehensweise wurde eine Charta verfasst, welche die Landwirtschaft in das Landschaftsprojekt integriert. Dieses Dokument legt gemeinsame Kriterien fest, um die verschiedenen landschaftlichen Elemente der landwirtschaftlichen Tätigkeit (Pflöcke, Gatter, Grabenbrücken) aufeinander abzustimmen. Die Prinzipien verstärken den Leitfaden des Projekts, welches in einer klaren, evolutionären Vorgehensweise ausgearbeitet wurde. Die Grünanlage stellt tatsächlich den ersten Bestandteil eines Systems auf Ebene der Metropole dar, von dem ausgehend andere Parks geplant werden. Das Landschaftsprojekt ermöglicht es, die Ordnung des Raums auf einer breiten Ebene zu überdenken. Das Grünsystem stützt sich auf eine deutliche Markierung der natürlichen Strukturen (Relief und Gewässer) sowie der anthropogenen Raumformen, um die neue Anlage der Stadtmetropole Lille klarer und kohärenter zu machen. Der Park hebt eine inszenierte Natur, um die drei verschiedenen Naturthemen strukturiert, hervor.

Akteurszusammenhänge

Schon im Jahr 1973 fand die Idee dieser Grünanlage Eingang in das Leitschema (Schéma Directeur) der Lille Métropole. Ab 1993 wurde das Projekt vom Gemeindesyndikat des Parc de la Deûle geleitet, in welchem die Lille Métropole und die Gemeinden Wavrin, Houplin-Ancoisne sowie Santes eingebunden sind. Die Organisation ging kurze Zeit später mit dem Team Simon & JNC International, das die Entwürfe im Jahr 1995 ausgearbeitet hat, einen Vertrag ein. Das Gemeindesyndikat profitierte auch von den technischen Kompetenzen der Abteilung Naturraum der Metropole des Büros für Stadtplanung und Stadtentwicklung von Lille. Die häufige und langfristige Inanspruchnahme dieses technischen Fachwissens parallel zur Gestaltung breiterer Gebietseinheiten waren Hauptvorteile für das Gelingen und die Erweiterung des Projekts. Ein anderer Erfolgsfaktor liegt in der Befragung der lokalen Akteure (Anwohner, Landwirte, Naturforscher, Politiker). Die örtliche Absprache hat zur Gründung eines Konsultativrats der Metropole geführt, in dem Landwirtschaftsgewerkschaften,

Naturschutzverbände, Freiluftsportvereine und Kulturvereinigungen versammelt sind. Im Jahr 1997 wurde der Park als Hauptprojekt in das Leitschema für die Entwicklung von Lille aufgenommen. Im Februar 1999 wurden 277 Hektar Gelände für gemeinnützig erklärt und die Bauarbeiten begannen. Der Parc de la Deûle trägt zur Strategie «Grünmetropole» (Métropole Verte) bei. Am Ende der 90er Jahre wurde im grünen Leitschema das Projekt vorgebracht, weite Flächen mit ökologischem Reichtum oder Erholungsqualitäten in einem breiten Grüngürtel zu vereinen. Im Rahmen einer Charta, welche die Absichten dieses Planungsdokuments und der Strategie «Grünmetropole» aufgreift, wurde von der Lille Métropole, dem Departement, der Region und dem Staat eine Verpflichtungserklärung unterzeichnet. Es wurde unter anderem das Ziel verfolgt, nach zehn Jahren über 10.000 Hektar Natur- und Erholungsgebiet auf Ebene der Metropole Lille zu verfügen. Das Gemeindesyndikat Naturräume Lille Metropole (Espace Naturel Lille Métropole) ist mit der Umsetzung dieser breiten grünen Infrastruktur beauftragt.

Finanzierungsrahmen

Innerhalb von zehn Jahren wurden, dank der investierten 23 Millionen Euro, 350 Hektar und 40 Kilometer Wege in den vier hauptsächlich betroffenen Gemeinden saniert oder angelegt; die «Ausbreitung» des Parks Richtung Norden und Süden dürfte letztendlich Lille mit Lens, um 2000 Hektar landwirtschaftliche und natürliche Flächen herum, verbinden. Hinter diesem Vorhaben steckt die Idee eines grünen und blauen Netzes. Darüber hinaus wird die Ambition einer europäischen landschaftlichen Vernetzung sichtbar, bei der Ökotourismus, Ökologie und Landwirtschaft auch innerhalb dicht bevölkerter Räume aufeinandertreffen.

Fazit

Den Parc de la Deûle, der vor den Toren der Stadt liegt, kann man mit einer städtischen Infrastruktur vergleichen, die in der Lage ist, sowohl die alltäglichen Bedürfnisse im Hinblick auf Erholungsräume für die anliegende Bevölkerung als auch den Wunsch nach Natur für alle Einwohner der Metropole zu befriedigen. Außerdem hat der Park eine ökologische Bedeutung (als Ausgleichfläche zur Klimaverbesserung und zur Förderung der biologischen Vielfalt), die den Nutzern nicht unmittelbar bewusst wird. Die drei Naturthemen – «wiedergefunden», «gezähmt» und «geträumt» – bilden den Leitfaden einer naturnahen gestalteten Landschaft, die eine Vielzahl an ausdrucksstarken Schauplätzen bietet: Industriebrachen, Feuchtgebiete, Wiesen, Felder, Hecken und Gräben, Gärten, Höfe und Spazierwege. Für die Stadtregion spielt der Parc de la Deûle eine strukturierende Rolle.

Lyon
Confluence

MURIEL DELABARRE

Innovativer Ansatz des Projektes

Das Projekt Lyon Confluence folgt der Logik einer Stadterneuerung nach innen auf einem ehemaligen Industrie- und Logistikstandort. Diese Revitalisierungsfläche im Süden der Lyoner Halbinsel ist ein zentraler Bereich der Stadt, der qualitativ aufgewertet und in der Fläche verdoppelt wird.

In der ersten Phase der Gebietsentwicklung (Gesamtfläche von 41,5 Hektar) soll im nördlichen Teil entlang des Flusses Saône ein funktional gemischtes Stadtviertel entstehen. Mit der Kombination von Wohnungen, Büros und öffentlichen Einrichtungen, die um einen zwei Hektar großen See angeordnet sind, wird ein innerstädtisch-heterogener Charakter angestrebt. Im Süden soll ein Freizeit- und Kulturzentrum entstehen, das Handels- und Dienstleistungsfunktionen bietet. Die Siedlung wird im Westen von einem Stadtpark gesäumt.

2010 begann die zweite Phase des Projektes, das auf einer Gesamtfläche von 35 Hektar Landschaft und Gebäude vernetzt. Anstelle des Großmarkts am Rhôneufer sollte ein dichtes und durchlässiges Stadtviertel entstehen, das die traditionelle rechteckige Form der Straßen aufnimmt und 30 Prozent der bestehenden industriellen Gebäude erhält und in das Projekt miteinbezieht. Die neuen Wohnblocks sind durchlässig angeordnet. Die Kombination verschiedener Gebäudehöhen und Gebäudetypen bringt viel Licht in die Gärten der Innenhöfe. Diese Raumkonzeption und das begleitende Grünkonzept mit Baumreihen, die zu einer guten Orientierung und Wahrnehmung beitragen, schaffen eine besondere Qualität für den öffentlichen Raum. Im Süden wird die Dichte des Stadtviertels durch eine klare Grenze unterbrochen, durch den Wohnpark Le Champ (das Feld). Der Park ist ein Teil des Gesamtsystems und erinnert an die ehemaligen landschaftlichen Windungen der Halbinsel. Das Stadtentwicklungsprojekt hat 2009 den «Preis der Ökoquartiere» («Palmarès des Écoquartiers») vom Ministerium für Ökologie in der Kategorie Städtische Dichte und Formen erhalten. Die Jury schätzte vor allem die Ausgewogenheit zwischen den dichten Wohnblocks und dem offenen Park.

Im Jahr 2000 wurde entschieden, einen Park als ein verzweigtes, mäandrierendes System zu planen, das sich entlang dem Strang des Flusses Saône schlängelt – ein spezifisches, den Park durchdringendes System von Pflanzen- und Wasserachsen, das sich in die Zwischenräume der Bebauung unterschiedlicher Gestalt und Dichte einfügt. Insgesamt zählt der 14 Hektar große Park 3280 hochstämmige Bäume. So soll eine Landschaft mit natürlichem Erscheinungsbild entstehen. Die Anpassungsfähigkeit und Flexibilität des Parks charakterisiert auch die Entwicklung des neuen Stadtviertels. Das Konzept «verzweigter Park» stützt sich vor allem auf eine enge Verzahnung von Natur und Behausung. Daher sah man Pflanzen und Böden vor, die sich an Wasser und Bauten anpassten. Dieser Park, der für die speziellen technischen Erfordernisse und für einen bestimmten Nutzungsbedarf gestaltet wurde, besteht daher aus einer Kombination von Wasseranlagen (Wassergräben, Hafenbecken und Wassergarten). Das neue Grün bezieht sich auf die räumlichen Spuren der Vergangenheit, indem es die Landschaft neu interpretiert.

Das Ausmaß des Projekts ermöglicht verschieden-
artige Naturformen:

• Die strukturierende Vegetation
In der ersten Phase von Lyon Confluence wurde
darauf geachtet, dass sich der verzweigte Park in
den Straßen bis in das Herz der Bebauung fort-
setzt, eine Vorgabe, die der Entwurf des Landschaftsplaners Michel Desvigne als «grüne Finger»
oder «Verästelung» interpretiert. In der zweiten Phase der Projektumsetzung sind die pflanzlichen Räume, trotz einer hohen Bebauungsdichte, besonders
wichtig: mit Gartenhöfen und Baumgruppen. Die
innovative Gestaltung der privaten Flächen macht
auch Bepflanzung möglich. Schließlich sieht diese
zweite Phase des Projekts die Gestaltung einer
neuen Art Wohnpark, Le Champ genannt, im äu-
ßersten Süden des Gebiets vor. Dieser Raum, von
in Lyon bisher unbekannter Form, wird von mit Bäu-
men eingesäumten Wassergräben durchzogen.
Obwohl die privaten Grundstücke den größten Teil
der Fläche des Le-Champ-Projekts ausmachen,
wird sich in diesem Bereich ein ausgedehnter öffentlicher Park befinden. Er soll einen Lebensraum
für mehrere Dutzend Tier- und Pflanzenarten bieten
und damit die ökologische Vielfalt sichern.

• Das aufgewertete Wasser
Lange Zeit wurden die Flüsse Rhône und Saône
wegen der häufigen Überschwemmungen vor allem als Gefahr wahrgenommen. Heute stellt der
Zugang zu den Flüssen in der Stadt eine neue urbane Qualität dar und das Naturerbe wird dadurch
aufgewertet. Im Zentrum des Parks wurde ein Hafenbecken vorgesehen, das das Wasser der Saône
bis zur Hauptader Cours Charlemagne fließen lässt
und Zugang zu einer Flussanlegestelle ermöglicht.
Dieses zwei Hektar große Becken dient außerdem
als Ort für Festveranstaltungen. Die Wassergärten, die auf beiden Seiten des Beckens gegraben
wurden, ergänzen das Angebot von Naturräumen,
die den Spaziergängern am Ufer der Saône zur
Verfügung stehen. Wiesen, Weiden, Waldflächen
und Wasserpflanzen bilden den Naturkomplex. Es
wurden nur robuste Pflanzenarten ausgewählt, die
sich unter dem Klima Lyons bewährt haben und
kaum Pflege brauchen. Diese Wasserflächen sind
als lebendige Ökosysteme entworfen, die Vegetation der Feuchtgebiete ist Lebensraum unter anderem für Enten und Libellen. Wassergräben führen
die ökologische Diversität bis in die Stadt hinein
und verstärken die Fortsetzung des ökologischen
Prinzips.

• Das verstärkte grüne und blaue Netz
Im größeren Maßstab werden die Vernetzungen dieser Wasserwege noch deutlicher: die Balmes de Sainte-Foy lès-Lyon am rechten Saôneufer und der Parc de Gerland an der Rhône. Das Projekt sieht ein «blaues Netz» um die Rhône und die Saône und ein «grünes Netz» entlang der Ufer vor. Entlang der Flüsse ist eine Baumallee für Fußgänger und ein Fahrradweg geplant.
Dieses Naturprojekt lehnt sich stark an die amerikanischen Parksysteme des 19. Jahrhunderts an, die oft strukturierend für das Städtewachstum gewesen sind. Die Parks von Frederick Law Olmsted

für Minneapolis und Boston, die die geografisch nicht besonders vorteilhaft gelegenen Städte deutlich aufwerten, haben die Designteams überzeugt, die Spuren in der Landschaft wichtig zu nehmen. In Lyon Confluence lässt sich die Entwicklung einer Ästhetik der Spuren aus der Vergangenheit durch die Gestaltung der Räume beobachten: Relikte der lokalen Geografie, eine Reihe von Infrastrukturen und ehemaligen Industriestandorten sind Gelegenheiten für die Rückeroberung dieses Bereichs.

dem Stadtplaner François Grether und dem Land-schaftsarchitekten Michel Desvigne, seine Ar-beit im Rahmen dieses Projekts begonnen. Seit 2002 steht SPLA das Planungsbüro Tribu als Bauherrenberater für nachhaltige Entwicklungs-ansätze zur Seite. Es soll Leitlinien entwerfen, die für das ganze städtebauliche Projekt gültig sind. Im Jahr 2007 wurde diese Nachhaltigkeitspers-pektive stärker berücksichtigt: Vor Beginn der zweiten Phase (Rhône) wurde sogar eine Nach-haltigkeitsbilanz erstellt. Die sich daraus ergeben-den Schlussfolgerungen wurden im Pflichtenheft der Projektgestalter festgehalten. Anschließend hat der Raumplaner eine innovative Vorgehens-weise für die Umsetzung des städtebaulichen Projekts auf den Weg gebracht. Er organisiert die Zusammenarbeit zwischen fünf Abteilungen mit sich ergänzenden Kompetenzen:

- Abteilung Stadtplanung, Landschaft und Archi-tektur: Herzog & de Meuron (Stadtplanung) und Michel Desvigne (Landschaftsgestaltung);
- Abteilung Programmplanung und Absprache: Initial Consultants und Sémaphores;
- Abteilung Straßen, Leitungsnetze und Mobilität: Opus, Girus, Item;
- Abteilung Nachhaltige Entwicklung: Tribu;
- Abteilung Belastete Standorte und Böden: Sogreah Magelis.

Alle diese Abteilungen berücksichtigen die Emp-fehlungen zur Nachhaltigkeit, die im Zentrum der Gesamtidentität von Lyon Confluence stehen. Lyon Confluence wurde im größeren Rahmen des Projekts «Grand Lyon» verwirklicht, welches seine gesamte Vorgehensweise in der lokalen Agenda 21 und durch seine örtlichen Aktionsplä-ne definiert hat. Dieses Projekt trägt zum Beispiel zur Eingliederung von Pflanzen im Stadtmilieu im Sinne der «Baumcharta» bei, zur Versickerung des Regenwassers in der Parzelle, zur Sanierung der belasteten Standorte und Böden sowie zu dem Ziel, die Treibhausgasemissionen zu senken, in Übereinstimmung mit dem Faktor Vier für den Ho-rizont 2050, wie im Klimaplan der Agglomeration festgelegt.

Es handelt sich um das erste nachhaltige Stadt-viertel in Frankreich, das nach den Richtlinien des vom World Wildlife Fund aufgestellten Kon-zepts «One Planet Living» gestaltet wurde. Ziel dieses bisher nur in neuen Projekten (zum Bei-spiel Bedzed im Süden Londons, Masdar in Abu Dhabi, dem Touristenkomplex Mata de Sesimbra in Portugal) erprobten Programms ist es, den öko-logischen Fußabdruck unserer Lebensstile (im Hinblick auf Energie, Wasser, Abfälle, Biodiversität)

Akteurszusammenhänge

Das Projekt wird von der Société Publique Locale d'Aménagement (SPLA), einer Partnerschaft, durchgeführt. Die SPLA Lyon Confluence hat die Umsetzung von Raumplanungsmaßnahmen und -programmen in diesem Gebiet zum Ziel. Sie ist für die Durchführung der Projektstudien, den Grund-erwerb, die Bauherrschaft der öffentlichen Räume, den Grundstücksverkauf an private Bauträger, die Gesamtkoordination der Bauarbeiten, die Abspra-che und die Kommunikation verantwortlich.

Im Jahr 2000 hat das Bauleitungsteam für die Konzeption der ersten Phase, bestehend aus

zu reduzieren und bis 2020 keine neuen Treibhausgasemissionen mehr zu verursachen.

Finanzierungsrahmen

Für den Zeitraum von 2003 bis 2016 wurden
177 Millionen Euro im Rahmen der öffentlichen
Raumordnungsvereinbarung investiert. Im Jahr
2006 wurde die erste Phase der Bauarbeiten auf
41 Hektar (40 Prozent der gesamten Projektflä-
che) begonnen. Die günstige Lage sowie neue
Einrichtungen und eine 250.000 Quadratkilometer große Fläche, die dem Dienstleistungssektor
gewidmet ist, haben Entscheidungs- und In-
vestitionsträger angesprochen; das Projekt zog
Großkonzerne wie Eiffage, GDF Suez, Cardinal
oder GL Events, der hier seinen Hauptsitz eingerichtet hat, an. Auch der Verwaltungssitz der
Region Rhône-Alpes befindet sich in diesem Stadtviertel. Insgesamt haben sich bis 2014 fast 7000
Arbeitnehmer in Lyon Confluence niedergelassen.
Das Projekt profitiert von der Anziehungskraft sei-
nes Freizeit- und Einkaufszentrums von Unibail-
Rodamco sowie seiner grünen Wohnblocks, die
von zwölf berühmten Architektenteams entworfen
wurden, um die Entscheidungs- und Investitions-
träger anzuziehen. Bis jetzt wurden 1,5 Milliarden
Euro investiert. 64 Prozent davon kommen aus
privaten Quellen.

Fazit

Das städtebauliche Projekt richtet den Fokus auf
die Spuren der Vergangenheit, die überkomme-
ne Landschaft. Anstatt die Leerräume mit neu-
en Strukturen zu füllen, gestaltet das Projekt mit
einfachen Mitteln eine neue Geografie: mittels der
Markierung von Spuren der ursprünglichen Landschaft, der Berücksichtigung der Bodenfrucht-
barkeit, der Ableitung des Regenwassers und der
Ausarbeitung eines neuartigen Managements zum
Unterhalt der Flächen. Die Verwirklichung der öffentlichen Räume der ersten Phase bildet Proto-
typen, die sich auf der ganzen Fläche verbreiten
sollen. Die untereinander verbundenen räumlichen
Maßnahmen bilden schließlich eine landschaftliche
Kontinuität, die sich in der Natur (Pflanzen, Wasser,
Biodiversität, Boden, Himmel und Sonne usw.) wi-
derspiegelt. Die umgesetzten räumlichen Konfigu-
rationen (wie zum Beispiel das Hafenbecken und
die Wassergärten) oder die noch zu erarbeitenden
Formen (Le Champ) sind nicht nur dazu bestimmt,
die materielle Entwicklung der Stadt und der Natur zu strukturieren. Sie wirken sich erheblich auf
die Wohnformen aus, indem sie die parzellierten
Wohnlagen aufwerten.

Deutschland
Finnland
Frankreich
Niederlande
Vereinigtes
Königreich

Breda
Au Fil de l'Eau

JENNIFER BUYCK

Innovativer Ansatz des Projektes

In Breda, der ehemaligen Hauptstadt der Provinz Noord Brabant, leben heute ca. 172.000 Einwohner. Die Stadt setzt seit 30 Jahren auf eine nachhaltige Stadtentwicklung, um sich gegenüber den direkten Nachbarstädten Rotterdam und Amsterdam zu profilieren. Sie gilt in Bezug auf umweltfreundliche und soziale Stadtentwicklungsansätze als Vorbild unter den europäischen Mittelstädten. Durch die Nutzung von Synergien der Vergangenheit und Gegenwart in den Bereichen Urbanität und Landschaft, Lebensqualität und qualitative architektonische Gestaltung sowie sanfte Mobilität und Freiraumgestaltung sticht die Stadt besonders durch folgende globale und integrative Herangehensweisen hervor:

- Ausgleich der Energiebilanz,
- Reduzierung von Müll- und Geruchsquellen,
- Erhöhung der Biodiversität,
- Orientierung der städtebaulichen Entwicklung an dem vorhandenen Kanal- und Flussnetz,
- Regenwasserbewirtschaftung,
- Erhaltung von Ruhezonen im öffentlichen Raum als Kontrast zur dynamischen Lebensweise,
- Verbindung von Freiräumen in der Stadt («Grüne Finger» erreichbar innerhalb einer Entfernung von ca. 200 Metern),
- Orientierung wirtschaftlicher Projekte am Prinzip der Nachhaltigkeit.

Diese Ziele, die alle räumlichen Maßstäbe betreffen (Stadtregion, Kommune und Quartier), sollen Attraktivität schaffen und dabei helfen, den Suburbanisierungsprozess zu kontrollieren. Die Stadt setzt weniger auf die Imagewirkung einer außergewöhnlichen Architektur als vielmehr auf die nachhaltige Entwicklung der Stadt und die Aufwertung ihrer Bestandteile. Die Stadtplanung folgt zudem der sogenannten care policy. Das Ziel des Projektes ist es, durch die Etablierung einer neuen, gemeinschaftlichen Urbanität, durch ein wachsendes Bewusstsein der Bürger für Themen wie Freiraum, Natur und «Wohnen in Gemeinschaft» sowie durch die (politische) Beteiligung lokaler Akteure eine größere Lebensqualität zu ermöglichen – im Gegensatz zu rein visionären Vorstellungen.

Aufgrund des hohen Risikos von Überschwemmungen, bedingt durch die zahlreichen Flüsse und Kanäle, verfolgt die Stadt Breda zwei Ziele: eine integrierte Regenwasserbewirtschaftung sowie den vorrangigen Schutz von Wasserrückhaltezonen. Um sich vor den Auswirkungen eines Hochwassers zu schützen, hat die Stadt ein Wasserschutzprogramm aufgestellt. Durch die Anlegung von Mäandern und die Verlegung von Flussläufen in ihr Ursprungsbett soll eine Renaturierung der Wasserläufe erreicht werden. Diese

Vorgehensweise trägt zum einen zum Schutz der vorhandenen Ökosysteme bei, gleichzeitig werden die grünen städtischen Freiräume für die Bürger erhalten.

Durch die Anlegung von Fuß- und Radwegverbindungen in den Wasserrückhaltezonen sollen neue Angebote für Radfahrer und Spaziergänger geschaffen werden. Ein Projekt zur Freiraumgestaltung ist zum Beispiel die Freilegung eines bisher kanalisierten Flusslaufes im Stadtzentrum.

Akteurszusammenhänge

Das Projekt vereint eine Vielzahl an Akteuren, etwa Fachleute und lokale Politiker, die sich über einen längeren Zeitraum hinweg für den Erfolg einsetzen. Diese Kontinuität hatte trotz politischer Veränderungen Bestand. Um eine gemeinsame Basis zu schaffen, sind differenzierte Betrachtungsweisen und Maßnahmen erforderlich: ein professioneller Stadtplan, die Betrachtung der Mobilitätsströme, die Gestaltung des öffentlichen

- Rinnen, die das Regenwasser in die Kanäle ableiten,
- Anlegen von Drainagen,
- Durchlässigkeit des Bodens und des Bodenbelags,
- Bepflanzung der Wasserränder und Kanäle,
- rasenbegrünte Becken,
- Wasserreservoirs.

Hinsichtlich Architektur und stadträumlicher Gestaltung entwickelt sich die Stadt Breda zukunftsorientiert. Insbesondere die Ideen für neue periphere Stadtquartiere, bei denen Aspekte der Vergangenheit und der Gegenwart verknüpft werden, sind von hoher Qualität. Der qualitative Anspruch bezieht sich dabei nicht nur auf einige Pilotprojekte, sondern ist ebenso ein wichtiger Faktor in der Gestaltung der öffentlichen Freiräume.

Finanzierungsrahmen

Ein wesentlicher Erfolgsfaktor der nachhaltigen Stadtentwicklungspolitik in Breda ist die Kooperation in Form von Public-Private-Partnership (PPP). Um ein Projekt dieser Art umzusetzen, gibt es keine besonders geeignete Stadtgröße. Es kommt vielmehr auf die Ambitionen und die Eigeninitiativen der einzelnen Akteure an – auch auf ihre Fähigkeit, ihr Handeln und sich selbst zu reflektieren. Diese Fähigkeiten sind eine wichtige Grundlage für Innovation und Kreativität. Außerdem erfordert die Kooperation in Form einer PPP Engagement und Kapital von mindestens zwei Akteuren. In diesem Fall handelt es sich um eine Win-win-Situation, die notwendig für eine nachhaltige Projektentwicklung und eine lokal angepasste Umsetzung ist.

Die Stadt Breda verfolgt eine sanfte Stadtentwicklung unter dem Aspekt der Nachhaltigkeit. Konkrete Ziele sind zum Beispiel: die Herstellung von Verbindungen zwischen dicht bebauten Räumen und Freiräumen, ein grundlegender qualitativer Anspruch in der Architektur, die Integration von sozialen Aspekten, «sanfte» (CO_2-arme) Mobilitätsformen und öffentliche Plätze, die als Ruhezonen dienen, sowie Kultur- und Freizeitangebote an die Bürger. Allerdings stehen nachhaltige Ansätze der wirtschaftlichen Entwicklung der Stadt nicht im Weg. Breda beweist, dass sich die Begriffe Nachhaltigkeit sowie soziale und wirtschaftliche Dynamik nicht gegenseitig ausschließen.

Ein interessantes Beispiel ist das Casino von Breda, das in einem Kloster aus dem 16. Jahrhundert untergebracht wurde. Die Stadt hat es für die Summe von einem Forint an einen privaten

Raumes, eine Fokussierung auf das Stadtzentrum und die Errichtung von neuen Quartieren.

Die Stadt Breda nimmt im Sinne der Governance eine Hauptrolle ein und garantiert damit den Zusammenhalt der verschiedenen Akteure. Außerdem haben die verschiedenen Maßnahmen des integrierten Wassermanagements der Stadt dazu geführt, dass eine breite Palette von technischen Alternativen zur Regenwassernutzung entwickelt wurde:

Investor verkauft, unter der Bedingung, dass dieser die denkmalgerechte Renovierung des Gebäudes übernimmt. Diese vertragliche Aktion war die einzige Möglichkeit, dieses städtische Denkmal vor dem Verfall zu retten – und setzte dabei gleichzeitig eine ökonomische Entwicklung in Gang, die heute 650.000 Besucher im Jahr nach Breda kommen lässt.

Fazit

Breda, auf Platz neun der großen Städte in den Niederlanden, gehört zu einer Reihe von Mittelstädten, die zwischen den beiden Attraktionszentren Antwerpen und Rotterdam angesiedelt sind. Gleichzeitig leidet Breda unter einer starken Luftverschmutzung, die von Rotterdam, Antwerpen, dem Ruhrgebiet und sogar aus England einwirkt. Grundsätzlich besitzt Breda wenige Attraktionen außer einigen historischen Denkmälern, die aber einem Vergleich mit Amsterdam oder Delft nicht standhalten können.

Trotz dieser Schwierigkeiten muss sich Breda weiterentwickeln können. Deshalb ist die Stadt gezwungen, Innovationen zu fördern und sich gegen negative Umwelteinflüsse zu schützen. Mit effizienten öffentlichen Transportsystemen und alternativen Energielösungen versucht Breda, die Bevölkerungszahl zu stabilisieren und sogar leicht zu erhöhen. Um sich von Rotterdam abzusetzen und nicht als dessen Vorstadt zu gelten, setzt Breda auf Eigenständigkeit mit einer guten Erreichbarkeit, hoher Lebensqualität und mit vielfältigen kulturellen und kommerziellen Angeboten.

Die Architektur in Breda überrascht den Betrachter nicht nur durch ihre Einheit, sondern auch durch besondere Lebensräume, wie zum Beispiel lange

Balkone, die über den Kanal herausragen, und die ökologischen Quartiere und deren Kanäle mit einer unglaublich reichhaltigen Vegetation. Dadurch entstehen lebenswerte und identitätsstiftende Stadtquartiere ohne Eitelkeit oder Provokation. Es handelt sich hier um eine herkömmliche städtische Situation, die ihre Qualität durch den besonderen Bezug zur Natur erhält.

Die Beziehung zwischen Stadt und Natur spielt auch auf der regionalen Ebene eine wichtige Rolle, insbesondere in Bezug auf die Probleme der Suburbanisierung. Auch auf dieser Ebene ist die Planungspolitik von Breda bemerkenswert. Sie orientiert sich an der Natur der Grenzen: einerseits an den vom Staat verordneten Siedlungsgrenzen und andererseits an den eigens bestimmten Abgrenzungen zur Natur. In den Niederlanden bestehen diese aus künstlich geschaffenen Poldern und kultivierten Flächen für die Landwirtschaft. So können sowohl «Natur» als auch «Stadt» ständig neu gestaltet werden.

In diesem kulturellen Kontext handelt der Gemeinderat von Breda mit dem Ziel, die Landwirtschaft auf seinem Territorium zu erhalten und gleichzeitig eine gewinnbringende Beziehung zwischen den Bedürfnissen der Bauern und denen der Städter zu etablieren. Die Grenzen der Urbanisierung sind zwar streng markiert, um Zersiedelung zu verhindern, bieten jedoch vielfältige Möglichkeiten zum Dialog zwischen Stadt und Natur (Ufer der Kanäle, pflanzliche Lärmschutzwälle, Grünkorridore und Grünanlagen im Stadtquartier). Diese Öffnung zum Grün und zur Natur stellt für Investoren ein gesuchtes Kapital, eine besondere Wertschöpfung für ihre Projekte dar.

Amsterdam
Borneo & Sporenburg

JENNIFER BUYCK

Innovativer Ansatz des Projektes

Amsterdam als Hauptstadt und größte Stadt der Niederlande ist auch das ökonomische und kulturelle Zentrum des Landes. Die Stadt wurde am Ende des 12. Jahrhunderts um ein halbrundes Kanalsystem errichtet. Seitdem hat sich die Stadt entlang der Mündung des Flusses Amstel entwickelt. Im historischen Zentrum von Amsterdam leben heute mehr als 700.000 Einwohner (eine Dichte von 33,6 Einwohnern/ha). Zu der Agglomeration von Amsterdam zählen ca. 2,3 Millionen Einwohner, was einer Dichte von 18 Einwohnern/ha entspricht. Die hohe Einwohnerdichte mit einer hohen Lebensqualität in Einklang zu bringen, ist in diesem Kontext keine einfache Sache. Die Umgestaltung der Inseln Borneo und Sporenburg ist in diesem Zusammenhang ein wichtiges Beispiel für die neuen Entwicklungen in der Stadt Amsterdam, die Risikovorsorge und Umfeldverbesserung kombinieren.

Der erste weltweit bekannte Bebauungsplan für Amsterdam ist der «Algemeen Uitbreidingsplan (AUP)» (General Urban Expansion Plan), der 1935 veröffentlicht wurde. Dieser Plan setzte einen generellen Rahmen für das Wachstum der Stadt bis zum Jahr 2000 und war die Basis für die räumliche Entwicklung der Stadt in den 70er Jahren. Seit 1970 sind mehrere Bebauungspläne gefolgt, die auf die neuen räumlichen und sozialen Anforderungen der Stadt antworteten.

Zwischen 1980 und 1990 wanderten Einwohner und Unternehmen aus dem Zentrum ab, um sich in den Satellitenstädten anzusiedeln. Der Plan «Die kompakte Stadt» (1985) hatte zum Ziel, diese urbane Expansion einzudämmen. Seit den 1990er Jahren ist die Anzahl der Einwohner in Amsterdam wieder angestiegen und viele Unternehmen haben sich angesiedelt: Die Stadt und ihre Umgebung bilden ein Städtenetz, welches eine urbane Region formt.

Seit 1991 entstanden weitere Pläne, die sich mit Umweltthemen befassten. Im Jahr 2003 hat Amsterdam einen neuen städtebaulichen Plan entwickelt: «Wählen sie die Urbanität». Sein Ziel ist es, die bereits bebauten Bereiche der Stadt intensiver zu nutzen (mehr Platz, um in der gleichen Stadt zu leben und zu arbeiten), indem zwei Konzepte angewendet werden: die «Räume des Marktes» (Bereiche des Austauschs von Produkten, Informationen und Service) sowie die «Räume des Treffens» (Bereiche, um mit anderen Personen zusammenzutreffen). In diesem Zusammenhang kann die Sanierung der Eastern Docks als das beste Beispiel für die Transformation eines industriellen Quartiers des 19. Jahrhunderts zu einem zeitgenössischen Wohnquartier angesehen werden. Das Programm der Sanierung umfasst 8000 Wohnungen für 17.000 Einwohner sowie Einzelhandel und Gewerbe. Bei diesem Projekt wurde große Aufmerksamkeit auf die soziale Mischung gelegt, die aufgrund der Kombination von Sozialwohnungen,

Mietwohnungen und dem Erwerb von Eigentum
entsteht. Die bedeutsamsten Teile dieses Projektes befinden sich auf den Inseln Sporenburg und Borneo.

Zwei andere Halbinseln (Java und KNSM) wurden bereits zu einem früheren Zeitpunkt neu gestaltet. Obwohl die Planung für Java und KNSM Ähnlichkeiten mit Sporenburg und Borneo aufweist, ist ihre Ausgestaltung unterschiedlich. Auf Java und KNSM besteht die Bebauung aus hohen, zusammenhängenden oder einzelnen Gebäuden. Auf Borneo und Sporenburg handelt es sich hingegen um Schichten von niedrigen Gebäuden, die die Landschaft betonen. Dazu kommen hohe, künstlerisch gestaltete Blöcke, die einen Akzent am Horizont setzen. «Hier entfaltet sich, in extremer horizontaler Form, eine neue Typologie, die auf dem Konzept der Hyperdichte basiert: ein Gewebe aus Einzel- und Reihenhäusern, aneinandergereiht an geradlinigen Straßen, Gräben mit homogener Bebauung, die die Handschriften der renommiertesten Architekten erkennen lässt, parallel zu ruhigen Gewässern mit Docks. Hier zeigt sich eine ‹minerale Konzeption› des Landschaftsplaners Adriaan Geuze, der den Masterplan und die architektonischen Vorgaben entworfen hat (…)» («Hyperdensity in Borneo Sporenburg», In: Lotus international. Nr. 108/2001, S. 39–45).

Akteurszusammenhänge

Die alte Hafenzone, welche im Osten der Docks, nahezu im Herzen von Amsterdam liegt, wurde zum Objekt vieler Projekte. Jedes Dock wurde einem Architekten zugeteilt: Jo Coenen ist mit der Insel KNSM und einem relativ konventionellen Planungsansatz beauftragt worden. Sjoerd Soeters hat die Insel Java mit einem postmodernen Ansatz beplant und Adriaan Geuze (West 8) hat sich für Borneo und Sporenburg interessiert – mit einem Ansatz, der die städtische Landschaft integriert.

Die Gruppe der niederländischen Architekten West 8 hat den Wettbewerb für die Umgestaltung der Inseln Borneo und Sporenburg in der Eastern Docklands Area von Amsterdam gewonnen. Zwischen 1992 und 2000 wurde eine ungenutzte Hafenzone zu einem neuen Stadtquartier mit 2500 individuellen Wohnungen und gemeinschaftlichen Wohnblöcken umgestaltet. Die Verantwortung lag bei NEX Deal BV und jedes Wohnhaus wurde von einem anderen Architekten realisiert.

Nachdem schon seit mehreren Jahren Forschung zur Entwicklung von suburbanen Räumen entlang des Ijsselmeers unternommen worden waren, suchte Amsterdam immer noch nach Flächen für das städtische Wachstum. Als erstes begann die Regierung, das ehemals mit Containern, Lagerhäusern und Bahnschienen belegte Gelände neu zu bebauen. Die Namen der Inseln Borneo und Sporenburg rühren aus ihrer vergangenen Funktion her: Die Halbinsel Borneo war der Hafen, an dem die Waren von der gleichnamigen indonesischen Insel ankamen und im Namen Sporenburg klingen noch die «Sporen», also die Schienen der Eisenbahn nach.

Finanzierungsrahmen

Aus ihrer Lage mitten im Hafen von Amsterdam ergibt sich für die beiden neuen Quartiere eine wassernahe Urbanität: Meer und Stadt gehen einen Dialog ein. Das Überschwemmungsrisiko wird durch blinde Fassaden im Erdgeschoss, höhergelegte Eingänge und Systeme der wasserdichten Verschließung gemindert. Diese in den Niederlanden gängigen Baumaßnahmen sind jedoch nicht immer im Einklang mit den gesetzlichen Vorschriften zur Risikovorsorge von Überschwemmungen.

Die Ursprünge des neuen Quartiers Borneo-Sporenburg stammen noch aus der Zeit vor dem 1993 aufgelegten niederländischen Wohnungs-bauprogramm VINEX. In einem gewissen Maße hat dieses Projekt schon damals die aktuelle Wohnungsbaupolitik überholt und neue Akzente geschaffen.

Im Finanzierungsrahmen spiegeln sich die gängigen Einflussfaktoren der Niederlande wider: der

Grundstücksvertrag (ein Vorabvertrag von VINEX), die Wohnung (eine Politik für den Erwerb von Eigentum und für soziale Mischung), die Finanzierungen (Methoden der Grundstücksnutzung, die auf Gewinn basieren) und die Akteure (Körperschaften und Partnerschaften). Die Verwaltung hat nur geringen Einfluss auf diese Entwicklung. Offensichtlich wird die Entwicklung von Wohngebieten in den Niederlanden stark vom sozialen und kulturellen Kontext bestimmt. Auch wenn der ökonomisch-politische Kontext die Art der Verwaltung und Finanzierung definiert, dominiert eine Politik, in der die soziale Mischung beachtet wird. Adriaan Geuze (West 8), der den städtebaulichen Plan sowie den architektonischen Masterplan für dieses Projekt entworfen hat, hat Doppelhaushälften in großer Dichte vorgeschlagen, um die große Nachfrage nach Einfamilienhäusern zu befriedigen und trotzdem eine rentable Nutzung der Flächen zu erreichen. Eine Einheit von 2500 Wohnungen stellt ein dichtes Netz dar (100 Einheiten pro Hektar), das punktuelle Elemente mit einer größeren Höhe enthält. Um das Erfordernis der Dichte und die Idee der Einfamilienhäuser zu vereinbaren, hat Adriaan Geuze neue Typologien der Wohneinheiten in einem Block erfunden und damit den niederländischen Reihenhaustypus radikal verändert. Hier ist der öffentliche Raum auf die Straße reduziert; die Häuser mit drei Etagen und Dachterrasse sind mit privaten Gärten ausgestattet, die zu abgegrenzten Terrassen oder Innenhöfen (Patio) werden. Dadurch bleiben trotz der Kompaktheit des städtischen Gefüges Durchlässigkeit und Transparenz gewahrt. Durch das besondere Verhältnis der Häuser zum Wasser, dessen Pegel nur wenige Zentimeter unter dem Erdgeschoss liegt werten sich Bebauung und Umwelt gegenseitig auf.

Fazit

Die Struktur der alten Docks wird bewahrt und kombiniert mit einer Folge von identischen Modulen, von einzelnen herausstechenden Häusern, von privaten Gärten und von Grünflächen. Ein neues, offenes Stadtviertel ist entstanden, das sich trotz seiner sehr hohen Dichte in seine natürliche Umwelt einfügt und eine Kontinuität von Grün und qualitätvollen öffentlichen Räumen herstellt.

Man erreicht sein Haus von der Straße aus auf direktem Weg, ohne Übergang. Indem der öffentliche Raum minimiert wird, wird ein maximaler individueller, privater Raum geschaffen. Es existieren keine halböffentlichen Räume, keine Hindernisse und keine Begrünung der Straße. Es gibt keine Übergangsräume außer der Haustür: Sobald man sein Haus verlässt, ist man im öffentlichen Raum. Die Repetition der Einfamilienhäuser in einer großen Struktur greift den Maßstab der Docks auf.

Die Allgegenwart des Wassers bildet ein Gegengewicht zu der Bevölkerungsdichte der Insel und verleiht der «Wasserstadt» eine vertraute und gleichzeitig spannungsreiche Atmosphäre. 50 Prozent jedes Grundstücks sind privaten Gärten oder Innenhöfen vorbehalten, sodass jedes Haus einen verborgenen Teil hinter der Fassade besitzt.

Die Entwicklung von Amsterdam beruht seit jeher zum großen Teil auf der Schaffung künstlicher Inseln; in diesem Fall sind die Inseln durch das Ausbaggern von Sand entstanden (Pancake-Methode). Der Grund der Inseln liegt bei ein bis zwei Meter über dem Meeresspiegel.

Mittels eines ehrgeizigen ökologischen Programms sollen die negativen Auswirkungen der extremen Dichte auf das Ökosystem minimiert werden, insbesondere durch die Schaffung eines Mosaiks aus grünen Inseln, die einen ökologischen Korridor darstellen.

Das Quartier der Eastern Docks präsentiert einen hohen Grad an gestalterischer Einheit und wahrt dennoch den Eindruck der Vielseitigkeit. Dies ist möglich durch eine Liste von Anforderungen, die die Architekten entwickelt haben:

- einheitliche Nutzung des Materials (Ziegelstein und Holz);
- Variationen in den Öffnungen konzipieren eine Serie, verändern sich aber durch ein Spiel mit den Modulen;
- neue Typen von Häusern mit drei Etagen, die, bei jeweils verschiedenen gestalterischen Konzepten, auf den traditionellen niederländischen Gebäudemaßen beruhen;
- das konstruktive Prinzip begünstigt eine Fassade zur Straße mit einem direkten Zugang und einer Garage an der Parzelle; zusätzlich hat jedes Haus einen inneren Raum mit doppelter Höhe, einen Innenhof und/oder einen Garten.

An drei Standorten ist der Rhythmus durch höhere Wohngebäude unterbrochen. Diese künstlerischen Blöcke fungieren als Wegmarken in der städtischen Landschaft: der Fountainhead von Steven Holl, der Walyis der Architekten Cie und der Pacman von Koen van Velsen. Sie beziehen sich auf andere große Gebäude in Amsterdam, binden die Landschaft visuell in die Stadt ein und öffnen gleichzeitig die Stadt zur Landschaft. Der Einzelhandel und die Gastronomie nehmen einen Großteil der Erdgeschosse sowie der Innenhöfe ein und bilden somit halböffentliche Räume.

Deutschland
Finnland
Frankreich
Niederlande
**Vereinigtes
Königreich**

East London
Green Grid

Innovativer Ansatz des Projektes

Die East London Green Grid bildet den Rahmen für die Planung der grünen Infrastruktur (Green Infrastructure) der East London Sub Region. Im größeren Maßstab ist die Grid auch Teil des Programms für die Stadtentwicklung und die Förderung der Lebensqualität des «Parklands Spatial Framework» von Thames Gateway. Es handelt sich hier um das größte Erneuerungsprogramm in Großbritannien. Es umfasst einen weiten, überregionalen Raum, der sich an beiden Ufern entlang der Themse flussabwärts über die drei Grafschaften Greater London, Kent und Essex erstreckt. In diesem Gebiet, das zwei Millionen Einwohner umfasst, summieren sich die schwersten Probleme (Arbeitslosigkeit, Armut, Bodenverschmutzung und schlechte Erreichbarkeit) von Großbritannien. Die grüne Infrastruktur soll nicht nur verschiedene natürliche oder bepflanzte Flächen vernetzen, sondern auch den Stadträumen eine Struktur geben – und nicht zuletzt einen Beitrag zur Bewältigung der verschiedenen Umweltherausforderungen wie zum Beispiel Überschwemmungen oder Klimawandel leisten.

Die East London Green Grid ist in sechs Unterbezirke aufgeteilt. Ein wichtiger Aspekt ist deren Vernetzung. Strategische Grünkorridore sollen die Stadtzentren und die Verkehrsknotenpunkte mit den wichtigsten Arbeitsmarktzentren und den großen Wohngebieten verbinden. Zentrale Elemente des Projektes sind Flussläufe, deren Uferflächen und Verbindungen mit dem Grüngürtel. Die Struktur dieser Infrastruktur zeigt den fraktalen Charakter des Londoner Gebietes und – in einem größeren Rahmen – des Südostens von England. Das knüpft an die Äußerungen von Richard Rogers oder Bernardo Secchi über die offenen Räumen innewohnende gestaltende Kraft an. Im Gegensatz zu einer Stadt, die von dem individuellen Verkehrsverhalten der mobilen Stadtbevölkerung geprägt ist, setzt sich eine grüne Infrastruktur durch, die wie ein Korsett zur Straffung der zergliederten Stadt wirkt.

Akteurszusammenhänge

Das Projekt East London Green Grid wird vom East London Green Grid Project Board, einer Partnerstruktur, durchgeführt. Ihre Mitglieder sind:

- die London Development Agency (Entwicklungsabteilung für Great London),
- das Department for Communities and Local Government,
- die zehn Boroughs (Gemeinden) des Londoner Ostens, die vom grünen Netz abgedeckt sind,
- das Thames Gateway London Partnership,
- das Thames Gateway delivery vehicles (eine lokale Agentur zur Stadtentwicklung),
- die Environment Agency,
- Natural England.

Die East London Green Grid basiert eher auf einer ganzheitlichen Vision als auf einem normativen Ansatz. Bestandteile dieser Vision sind eine dezentralisierte Planung und ein individuelles Management, die an lokale Prioritäten und Strategien angepasst sind. Die Vision stützt sich auf zwei Dokumente des London Plan (ein Planungsinstrument für Greater London):

- den East London Green Grid Primer (ein Plan, der Kommunikationszwecken dient und 2006 veröffentlicht wurde),
- die East London Green Grid Framework Supplementary Planning Guidance (ein Planungsdokument, das 2008 veröffentlicht und mehrfach aktualisiert wurde).

Das zweite Dokument, das für Greater London ausgearbeitet wurde, ist die Supplementary Planning Guidance (SPG), die die East London Green Grid auf der infra-regionalen Ebene ausrichtet. Sie bestimmt die Richtlinien für die lokale Stadtplanung wie zum Beispiel die «Local Development Frameworks», «Open Space Strategies», «Regeneration Frameworks», die Masterpläne oder Bauanträge.

- Diese Richtlinie hat eine wichtige Auswirkung auf die Umsetzung der Vision. Sie gewährleistet unter anderem die Beteiligung der zehn betroffenen Boroughs Londons. Der Borough Tower Hamlets zum Beispiel hat sich die Entwicklung einer Green Grid zum Ziel gesetzt und hält dieses in seinen «Key Spatial Themes», im Rahmen seiner Core Strategy fest.
- Die Richtlinie schlägt darüber hinaus vor, dass die «Joint Development Plan Documents» oder die «Area Action Plans» für alle sechs Bezirke (abgedeckt durch die East London Green Grid Area) ausgearbeitet werden sollen. Diese Maßnahmen sollen die Biodiversität schützen sowie die Erreichbarkeit, die Vernetzung und die Qualität der Parks, der Erholungsgebiete, der offenen Räume sowie der Flüsse verbessern. Für jedes der sechs Areale, die in der Grid gegründet wurden, sind jeweils ein lokaler Präsident und ein Führungskomitee verantwortlich.

Finanzierung
Die Realisierung des vorläufigen Programms der Green Grid wird voraussichtlich mindestens 25 Jahre dauern und Investitionen in Höhe von mehr als einer halben Milliarde Pfund erfordern; davon wurden 80 Millionen Pfund bereits aufgebracht. Rund 300 Projekte wurden ausgewählt,

70 davon wurden von der London Development Agency als vorrangig betrachtet und auf der Basis ihrer Machbarkeit unterstützt. Die Projekte, die sich am leichtesten realisieren lassen, sind diejenigen, die auf einem bestehenden Managementsystem und einer lokalen Führung aufbauen. Auch Großprojekte spielen – insbesondere für die Freigabe von beachtlichen Fonds für Investitionen – eine wichtige Rolle. Das Projekt Erith Marshes and Belvedere Links, entlang der Themse im Borough von Bexley, zielt zum Beispiel darauf ab, eine der größten ehemaligen Industriezonen in ein nachhaltiges Arbeitsmarktzentrum zu verwandeln. Das Projekt wurde erarbeitet, um die Überschwemmungsrisiken zu reduzieren, die Umweltqualität der Feuchtzone Erith zu verbessern und um in dieser Zone (229 Hektar) zwischen 5000 und 10.000 neue Arbeitsplätze zu schaffen. Die wesentlichen Maßnahmen sind die Aufwertung der frei zugänglichen Räume und des Netzwerks von Dämmen, die

Entwicklung von nachhaltigen Entwässerungssystemen sowie die Verbesserung der Fuß- und Fahrradwege. Dafür wurden rund 10,6 Millionen Pfund durch das Communities and Local Government Parklands Program und den European Regional Development Fund aufgebracht. Außerdem wurden zwei Millionen Pfund von der London Development Agency beigetragen.

Besonderheiten
Die Analyse der East London Green Grid zeigt deutlich die aktuelle Richtung der strategischen Planung. Dieses Projekt geht von der Idee aus, dass Grünelemente im Raum die Fähigkeit besitzen, das Gebiet der Zwischenstadt zu gestalten. Es nutzt die offenen Räume als Struktur, um die Funktionen, die bis dahin von den Straßennetzwerken der modernen Stadt erfüllt wurden, zu gewährleisten. Außerdem spiegelt sich in der Umsetzung der East London Green Grid die Suche nach dem

richtigen Maßstab für die Entwicklung metropolitaner Räume. Dabei sollen die neuen grünen Infrastrukturelemente einen besonderen räumlichen Zusammenhalt bieten. Generell gesagt, ist das Projekt der zeitgenössischen Stadt vor allem ein Projekt, das im Boden verankert ist und zugleich dem aufgelockerten, fragmentierten und vielfältigen Ballungsraum einen Sinn gibt. Tatsächlich schafft diese neue Art von Grünprojekt eine neue Verbindung der verschiedenen Teile der Stadt. Restflächen werden aufgewertet und erhalten eine orientierende Bedeutung in einem grünen Gesamtplan. Diese Struktur erzeugt Situationen, in denen sich eine neue urbane Ästhetik erkennen lässt.

Die Initiative kombiniert verschiedene politische Ebenen und regt damit dazu an, das klassische System der Regierungsführung zu überdenken. Ein zentrales Anliegen des Projektes ist es, die Investitionen nach dem Projektstart dauerhaft zu sichern. Dabei ist die Frage nach einem langfristigen Management entscheidend, insbesondere im Kontext begrenzter Kompetenzen und Mittel. Die Lasten können infolgedessen nicht nur auf den lokalen Behörden ruhen. Aus diesem Grund hat die Greater London Authority während der Ausarbeitung der Supplementary Planning Guidance erkannt, dass es wichtig ist, schon mit Beginn eines Projekts eine langfristige Finanzierung zu sichern. Die Richtlinie Supplementary Planning Guidance empfiehlt die Eingliederung der East London Green Grid in die lokalen wirtschaftlichen Planungs- und Entwicklungsrichtlinien. Auf diese Art und Weise sind die örtlichen Behörden in Zukunft besser in der Lage, den Projektträgern dabei zu helfen, das Projekt East London Green Grid zu realisieren, zu verbessern und zu steuern. Von Anfang an soll auch der zukünftige Unterhalt der Flächen eingeplant werden. Diese Art von Antizipation vor dem Projektstart ist eine Grundvoraussetzung für die Freigabe der Finanzierungsfonds durch die Greater London Authority.

London
Greenwich
Millennium
Village

CHARLES AMBROSINO

Innovativer Ansatz des Projektes

Das Greenwich Millennium Village auf der Greenwich Peninsula in Greenwich, London ist das größte nachhaltige Stadtplanungsprojekt in Großbritannien (30 Hektar) und setzt sich als Modell der ökologischen Bauweise im ganzen Land durch. Der schwedische Architekt Ralph Erskine hat den Masterplan entworfen und den ersten Bauabschnitt der Wohnungen erarbeitet. Jeder Abschnitt ist um eine, wie es scheint, neue Version des Londoner Square angeordnet und von einem 13 Hektar großen grünen Herzstück, in dem sich zwei künstlich angelegte Seen und ein Ökopark befinden, umgeben. Das Projekt ist mit der Themse und der übrigen Halbinsel durch Grünkorridore und Naturwege verbunden. Zehntausende Bäume, Büsche und neue Graslandschaften wurden auf dieser ehemaligen Weide- und Teichlandschaft angepflanzt. Dieser breite, offene und zentrale Raum erfüllt verschiedene Funktionen, wie zum Beispiel öffentliche Zierfläche, Freizeitraum und Ort zur Sensibilisierung von Erwachsenen und Kindern für die Umwelt und zur ökologischen Bildung der Bevölkerung. Röhrichte und kleine Inseln wurden neu angelegt, um Vögel anzulocken und ihnen einen geschützten Lebensraum zu bieten. Außerdem wurden elf Millionen Pfund investiert, um den Tidebereich der Themse mit einem innovativen System von Terrassenanlagen am Flussufer zu verbessern.

Die Halbinsel von Greenwich, eine der wichtigsten Londoner Industriebrachen, steht kurz davor, revitalisiert zu werden. Im Osten der Docklands gelegen, beherbergte sie früher auf 121 Hektar die Betriebsanlagen der britischen Gaskompanie. Der Standort bietet aufgrund seiner Lage an der Themse und seiner Zentrumsnähe ein hohes Entwicklungspotenzial für Wirtschaft, Wohnfunktionen und Tourismus. Im Übrigen ist die Halbinsel heute einer der wichtigsten strategischen Bezirke (Opportunity Areas), die im London Plan (Raumentwicklungsstrategie für Greater London) erfasst wurden. Bis zum Jahr 2016 sollen hier 16.000 Arbeitsplätze geschaffen und 7500 Wohnungen gebaut werden. Im Rahmen eines größeren Stadtentwicklungsprojekts, „Thames Gateway", wurden die Leitlinien der Stadtsanierung für die Halbinsel festgelegt. Bevor die Regionalplanungsbehörde die Halbinsel als geeignetes

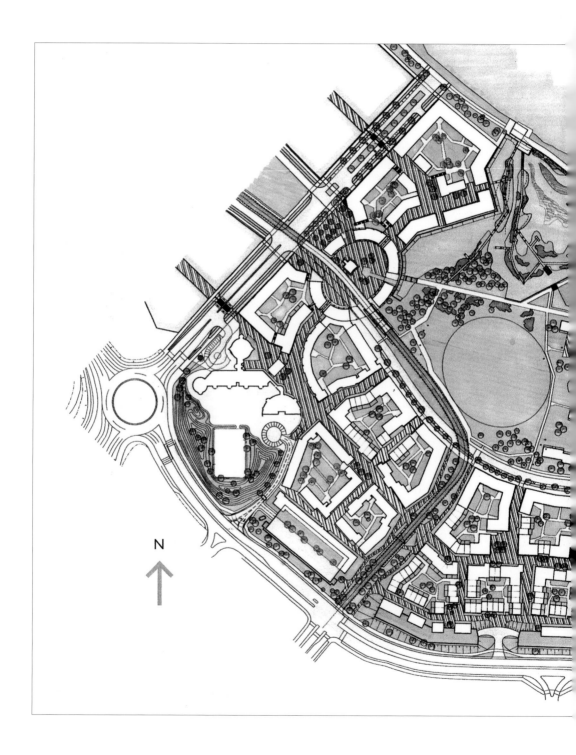

N

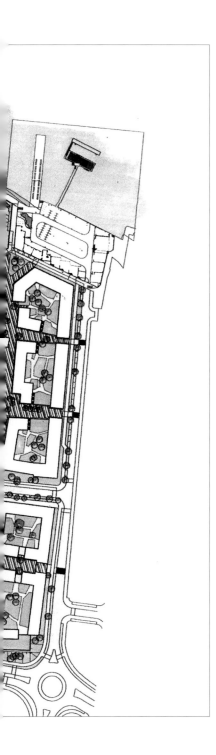

Gebiet für eine nachhaltige Stadtentwicklung aner-
kannte, musste das Projekt verschiedene Phasen
durchlaufen. Das Zögern der Behörden kann unter
anderem mit den erheblichen Kosten der Bodensanierung, der geografischen Isolation und der
mangelnden Verkehrsinfrastruktur erklärt werden.
Zu den wichtigsten geplanten Stadtentwicklungs-
projekten zählt das Millennium Village im Südosten
der Halbinsel. Die Bauträger des neuen Stadtviertels, Taylor Woodrow und Countryside Properties
PLC, wurden 1997 nach einer europäischen Ausschreibung ausgewählt. Die Ausschreibung fand im
Rahmen des „Millennium Communities Program"
von English Partnerships mit Beteiligung der nationalen Stadtsanierungsagentur und der Grundei-
gentümer statt. Auswahlkriterien waren die Qualität
der Architektur, der Landschaftsgestaltung sowie
die finanzielle Leistungsfähigkeit. Daraufhin wurde
die Gesellschaft Greenwich Millennium Village Ltd.
gegründet, die mit Projektpartnern für den sozialen
Wohnungsbau, der Moat Housing Group und Ujima
Housing, zusammenarbeitete.
Die von Ralph Erskine entworfenen Wohnungen
fördern die Energieeffizienz und die soziale Durch-
mischung. Das Village wird ungefähr 2520 Wohnungen in Form von Wohnanlagen und Stadt-
häusern aufweisen, davon werden 20 Prozent
ausdrücklich als „bezahlbarer Wohnraum" ausge-
wiesen werden. Die Gebäude sind so angeordnet,
dass die Wind- und Sonnenexposition maximiert
werden; damit sind Heizungs-, Warmwasser- und
Stromverbrauch optimal auf die Bedürfnisse der
Bewohner ausgerichtet. Die Entwicklungsziele
fördern eine deutliche Reduzierung des Energie-
verbrauchs (80 Prozent) durch die Nutzung von
energiesparenden Materialien und Geräten. Neben den Wohnungen wurden von der Gesellschaft
Greenwich Millennium Village Ltd. mehrere öffentliche Einrichtungen (Schulgebäude und Gesund-
heitskomplexe) sowie die Gestaltung und Pflege
einer Uferpromenade entlang der Themse und alle
öffentlichen Räume finanziert.

Akteurszusammenhänge

Im Auftrag der Bauherren Taylor Woodrow und
Countryside Properties PLC hat Ralph Erskine
detaillierte Gestaltungsrichtlinien für das Projekt
entworfen, den „Greenwich Millennium Village
Masterplan Design Code". Damit sollen alle Akteure in die gemeinsame Arbeit an einer klaren
gestalterischen Vision des Millennium Village eingebunden werden. Die im Design Code artiku-
lierten Schlüsselstrategien für die stadtplanerische

und landschaftliche Konzeption sind offen genug gehalten, um Verhandlungen mit den zukünftigen Baufirmen zu ermöglichen. Dazu gehören:

• Die stadtplanerischen Strategien:
Der „Design Code" unterscheidet verschiedene „räumliche Sequenzen". Damit soll eine Hierarchie etabliert werden, die verschiedene Räume mit unterschiedlichen Funktionen definiert. Das Dokument unterscheidet vier Arten von Räumen: den zentralen Park, die Kommunikations- und Verkehrsachsen, die öffentlichen Squares und die Innenhöfe der Wohnblöcke mit halbprivat-halböffentlichen Bereichen. Damit soll eine bessere Nutzungsmischung des städtischen Raums ermöglicht werden (zum Beispiel öffentliche und halböffentliche Nutzungen als Übergangszonen zwischen Öffentlichkeit und Privatheit im Erdgeschoss und im ersten Stock der Wohngebäude und der Stadthäuser).

• Die landschaftsplanerischen Strategien:
Mithilfe des Design Codes soll der Status der Räume geklärt und ein Angebot von vielfältigen Stadtsituationen gesichert werden. Es werden fünf Arten von Räumen unterschieden: der Oval Square, die Community Squares and Spaces, die Spine Streets, die Side Streets und die Courtyards. Für jede dieser Raumsequenzen werden Empfehlungen hinsichtlich der Pflanzungen, der Bodengestaltung, der Beleuchtung und der Stadtmöbel gegeben und mit Plänen, Schnitten und Referenzen verdeutlicht.

Finanzierungsrahmen

Der Trust for Urban Ecology (TRUE) ist seit 2002 für das Gesamtmanagement des Greenwich Peninsula Ecology Park, der früher im Besitz der English Partnerships war, verantwortlich. Dieser Trust stellt zwei Verantwortliche für diesen Park in Vollzeitbeschäftigung zur Verfügung. TRUE ist eine Unterabteilung für Stadtökologie des Wohlfahrtsverbands The Conservation Volunteers (TCV), einem wichtigen Akteur im Bereich der Ökologie und der Erhaltung des Umwelterbes. TRUE hat für seine Parks die folgenden Managementgrundsätze entwickelt:

• Die Stadtfauna soll einen neuen Lebensraum bieten;
• der Park soll eine Sensibilisierung für die Stadtökologie ermöglichen;
• für die Stadtbewohner und insbesondere für Schüler soll die Möglichkeit geboten werden, die Natur zu genießen und sie durch praktisches Experimentieren kennenzulernen;

- der Wert der „kreativen Instandhaltung" als ökologischer Ansatz zur Schaffung neuer Landschaf-
  ten soll bewiesen werden.

Fazit

Die Umsetzung des Greenwich Millennium Village
hat ihren Ursprung in einem relativ funktionalen
Verständnis von Stadtnatur und folgt verhältnis-
mäßig klassischen Zielen der nachhaltigen Stadtplanung. Die ökologische Funktion des Gebiets
wird sowohl durch die Energieeffizienz der Wohnungen als auch durch die Realisierung offener
Räume gewährleistet. Sie sind dazu bestimmt,
das Gebiet der Halbinsel besser zu gestalten
und die Fauna und Flora am Ufer der Themse zu
schützen.

Hier begleitet die Natur, stärker als im übrigen
Raum London, ein Projekt der städtebaulichen
Verdichtung, das Mehrfamilienwohnhäusern und
Wohnblöcken in einem Land, das diesen Wohnformen aus kulturellen Gründen mit Vorbehalt
begegnet, zur Akzeptanz verhelfen soll. Auf der
Ebene der Stadtregion spielt der Ökopark in jedem Fall eine strukturierende Rolle für die Umwelt und integriert sich in die East London Green
Grid. Der deutlich in den Vordergrund gestellte
gesellschaftlich relevante Ansatz des Leitungsor-
gans des Parks, die Art der angebotenen Aktivitäten und seine ästhetische Attraktivität machen
aus dem Ecology Park einen Ort, an dem es
möglich ist, neue Erfahrungen zu sammeln und
aus ihnen zu lernen.

Das Projekt kombiniert die Sensibilisierung für
die Natur mit der Kommunikation ökologischer
Themen, was sich nicht nur positiv auf seine
landschaftsplanerische Inszenierung und seinen
ökologischen Mehrwert auswirkt, sondern ihm
auch ein innovatives Image verleiht.

Grün in der Stadt
Stadt am Wasser

Die traditionelle Rolle des städtischen Grüns verändert und erweitert sich. Grüne Flächen sind nicht nur ein ästhetisches Element der Stadtverschönerung; sie erhalten in den untersuchten Fallbeispielen vielfältige neue, raum- und sozialstrukturierende Funktionen. Aus der Auswertung von Literaturrecherchen, Akteursbefragungen und Projektanalysen zu den zehn hier vorgestellten Fallbeispielen lassen sich die folgenden fünf zentralen Erkenntnisse ableiten:

Grün wird zum raumstrukturierenden Element in Stadt- und Regionalplanung

Die Verbindung fragmentierter Grünzonen in einem regionalen und städtischen Zusammenhang schafft neue räumliche Ordnung und Orientierung. In den englischen Projekten London Green Grid und Greenwich Millennium Village ist die Vielfalt der grünen „Rest"-flächen Ausgangspunkt für ein neues Netzwerk, das die bislang unverbundenen Stadträume physisch und perzeptiv in ein erfahrbares Territorium der Metropole London einbindet. Eine planerische Konzeption, die die unterschiedlichen räumlichen Ebenen (Makro-, Meso-, Mikro-) interaktiv betrachtet und neue Zusammenhänge aufzeigt, hat auch Einfluss auf die zeitliche Organisation der Planung: Weites Vorausdenken in möglichen Szenarien und antizipatives Vorgehen (Veränderungen einplanen) bringt nachhaltige Entwicklung.

Grün als Vektor für integrative Governance-Formen

Die Kommunikation zwischen Politikern, Experten und Endnutzern (Bewohner, Bürger, Besucher, Interessierte) ist eine wichtige Voraussetzung sowohl für eine allgemein akzeptierte Planung als auch für das Verständnis der speziellen Nutzungsformen und der Pflegenotwendigkeiten. Beim Landschaftspark Stuttgart wurde die Voraussetzung dafür zum Beispiel durch neue gesetzliche Vorgaben geschaffen. Das Land Baden-Württemberg ermöglichte den am Projekt beteiligten Kommunen den Zusammenschluss zum Verband Region Stuttgart. Dieses neu geschaffene Regionalparlament gibt den Bürgern eine stärkere Legitimität und schafft gleichzeitig Freiräume für integrative Planungsformen (Workshops, Focus Groups, Testplanungen, etc.). Ein ergebnisoffener Dialog sowie die zielgerichtete Anwendung und Kombination formeller und informeller Beteiligungsformate tragen wesentlich zur Akzeptanz und zur nachhaltigen Nutzung von Grünprojekten bei.

Grün als Amenity Attractor

Im Rahmen der Debatte um nachhaltige Stadtentwicklung ergibt sich eine Vielfalt neuer Arten und Funktionen des Grüns in der Stadt. Grünflächen und Vegetation, die eine technische Funktion in der Stadtökologie besitzen (Wassermanagement, Klimaschutz, Bodenerhaltung etc.), können gleichzeitig Räume und Materialien für attraktive Nutzungen oder angenehme Sinneserfahrungen bieten. Die Erfahrungen der Stadt Breda in den Niederlanden und der Stadt Kotka in Finnland mit der Wahrnehmung und der Aneignung von grünen Grenzbereichen zwischen Stadt und Industrie sowie Stadt und Umland machen deutlich, in welchem Maße herkömmliche Grünflächen eine besondere Qualität und Attraktivität für Investoren darstellen können. Der multifunktionale Charakter ökologischer Grünelemente in der Stadt hat Einfluss darauf, wie in der Stadt gelebt, wie ihre Räume genutzt werden. Die neugeschaffenen grünen Annehmlichkeiten bieten einen Mehrwert, der Investoren und neue Bürger anziehen kann.

Grün hilft, neue lokale Wirtschaftsformen zu initiieren

Grüne Leuchtturmprojekte, wie zum Beispiel Kotka in Finnland und Sporenburg in den Niederlanden können erhebliche Anschubkraft für die Belebung der lokalen Wirtschaft haben und wesentlich dazu beitragen, die Attraktivität des Standortes, insbesondere für potenzielle Investoren, zu steigern. Komplementär dazu können kleinteilige progressive Ansätze der Grüngestaltung, wie beispielsweise in Leipzig und Lille, das Bild eines Stadtteils verändern (Vorstellungen der Bürger und Besucher) und ein Impuls für die lokale ökonomische Entwicklung sein. Grünpolitik kann dazu beitragen, neue lokale Wirtschaftsformen zu schaffen. Die Finanzierung ist dabei mehr und mehr antizipativ und partnerschaftlich.

Deutschland
Region Stuttgart

Verband Region Stuttgart: Sitzungsvorlage Nr. 140/2004, Stuttgart 21.07.2004

Verband Region Stuttgart: Sitzungsvorlage Nr. 24/2005, Stuttgart 27.04.2005

Verband Region Stuttgart: Sitzungsvorlage Nr. 639/2008, Stuttgart 12.11.2008

Verband Region Stuttgart: Sitzungsvorlage Nr. 113/2010, Stuttgart 07.09.2010

Verband Region Stuttgart – Körperschaft des öffentlichen Rechts: Die Landschaftsparks in der Region Stuttgart.

http://www.landschaftspark-region-stuttgart.de, 22.09.2014

http://www.region-stuttgart.org/fileadmin/regionstuttgart/04_Informationen_und_Download/04_01_Veroeffentlichungen/04_04_01_Broschueren_und_Faltblaetter/landschaftspark_neckar_d.pdf, 22.09.2014

http://www.region-stuttgart.org/fileadmin/regionstuttgart/04_Informationen_und_Download/04_01_Veroeffentlichungen/04_04_01_Broschueren_und_Faltblaetter/landschaftspark_rems.pdf, 22.09.2014

http://www.region-stuttgart.org/fileadmin/regionstuttgart/04_Informationen_und_Download/04_01_Veroeffentlichungen/04_04_01_Broschueren_und_Faltblaetter/VRS_Landschaftspark_Albtrauf_Freigabe.pdf, 22.09.2014

Quartier an der Weißen Elster/am Karl-Heine-Kanal, Leipzig

Dezernat Stadtentwicklung und Bau Leipzig (Hg.): Konzeptioneller Stadtteilplan für den Leipziger Westen KSP West. Beiträge zur Stadtentwicklung (Bd. 44), S. 1–54

Stadt Leipzig: Forum Leipziger Westen. http://www.leipziger-westen.de/front_content.php?idart=225, 22.09.2014

Stadt Leipzig: Fördergebiete Leipziger Westen. http://www.leipzig.de/bauen-und-wohnen/foerdergebiete/leipziger-westen/efre-leipziger-westen, 17.11.2014)

Vielen Dank an:

Herrn Manfred Meister vom Verband Region Stuttgart,

Frau Elke Horstmann, Stadt Leipzig, Stadtplanungsamt – Planungsabteilung West

Finnland
Helsinki

Eronen, Matti: „The Green Fingers of Helsinki in Finland – A Green structure as a part of master planning". In: Werquin, Ann Caroll et al.: Green structure and urban planning – final report. Luxembourg 2005, S. 352–358

Gordon, Douglas: „Helsinki: CITY" u. „Helsinki: CITY-REGION". In: Gordon, Douglas (Hg.): Polymetrex North-South Interface. http://www.eurometrex.org/Docs/PolyMetreX/rina/rina18/en_helSInkl_north-South_flnal.pdf, Helsinki 2007, S. 11–44

Gordon, Douglas/Manninen, Rikhard/Veltheim, Olavi (Hg.): From City to City-Region – City of Helsinki Strategic Spatial Plan. http://www.hel.fi/hel2/ksv/julkaisut/julk_2009-8.pdf, Helsinki 2009

Hannikainen, Matti O.: Classification of Green Spaces in Helsinki and Vantaa – Full Report of the „Green Issues" Project. http://greenspace-issues.files.wordpress.com/2013/03/greenspace-hannikainen.pdf, Helsinki 2013

Helsinki City Planning Department/Environmental Office: Green areas system in Helsinki. http://www.kirjavasatama.fi/pdf/southharbour_greenareassystem_helsinki.pdf, 2002

Huhdanmaki, Aimo/Dubois-Taine, Geneviève: „Extension of Helsinki Region – Inner City, Edge City, Outskirts". In: Dubois-Taine, Geneviève (Hg.): European Cities. Insights on Outskirts. From Helsinki to Nicosia. Paris, S. 97–121

Jaakkola, Maria: „Helsinki, Finland: Greenness and Urban Form". In: Beatley, Timothy (Hg.): Green Cities of Europe – Global Lessons on Green Urbanism. Washington, D.C. 2012, S 109–128

Michalek, Michael: Helsinki, Finland: Close to the Forest, Nature in the City. http://depts.washington.edu/open2100/Resources/1_OpenSpaceSystems/Open_Space_Systems/helsinki.pdf, 2006

Organisation for Economic Cooperation and Development: Territorial Reviews: Helsinki, Finland. Paris 2003, S. 236

Vähä-Piikkiö, Inker/Maijala, Olli: „Helsinki". In: Werquin, Ann Caroll et al.: Green structure and urban planning – final report. Luxembourg 2005, S. 163–169

City of Helsinki: http://www.hel.fi/www/helsinki/en, 22.09.2014

Greater Helsinki Vision 2050 – International Ideas Competition, Jury Protocol, 15th December 2006 – 31th May 2007, 100 p.

Kotka

Antilla, Eija: „Meripuisto pokkasi palkinnon". Kymen Sanomat, 13.09.2012, S. 4–5

European Landscape Contractors Association (2012): „International ELCA Trend Award ‚Building with Green' presented to a Finnish Project: Katariina Beach Park in the Port City of Kotka honoured". http://www.szuz.cz/UserFiles/File/trend_award_release_2012.pdf, 22.09.2014

Flander, Jukka-Pekka: „The Finnish National Urban Park (NUP) Concept as Part of Sustainable Urban Planning". In: Veltheim, Taina/Pajari, Brita (Hg.): Forest Landscape Restroation in Central and Northern Europe. Joensuu 2005, S. 139–144

Kosko, Juha: „Huippupalkinto Meripuistolle". Kaupunkilehti Ankurri, 12.09.2012

Kotkan kaupunki: Welcome to Kotka! http://www4.kotka.fi/matkailu-lomakkeet/ kotka_english_web.pdf, Kotka 2008, S. 44

Kotkan kaupunki: Kotkan Kansallinen Kaupunkipuisto – Perustamis-selvitys. http://www.visitkotka.fi/instancedata/prime_product_julkaisu/kotka/embeds/visitkotkawwwstructure/16993_kkp_2013_web.pdf, Kotka 2013, S. 92

Leskinen, Pekka: „Katariinan Meripuisto Kotkassa on Vuoden 2012 ympäristörakenne". In: Betoni. Nr. 3/2012, http://www.betoni.com/Download/23785/bet1203_44-49.pdf, S. 44–49

Ojansivu, Merja: „MERI JA TUULI hallitsevat Katariinan Meripuistoa". In: Kuntatekniikka. Nr. 1/2013, http://lehti.kuntatekniikka.fi/sites/default/files/kt0113-PDf-WWW-hQ.pdf, S. 6–11

Leverage from the EU for Finnish environmental Projects: „The Empress's Park becomes the people's park". In: Leverage from the EU – European Union structural funds 2007–2013. http://www.rakennerahastot.fi/rakennerahastot/tiedostot/esitteet/rakennerahasto_englanti.pdf, S. 3

Vielen Dank an:

Frau Elina Nummi (Projektmanagerin für das Public Works Department Streets and Parks Division der Stadt Helsinki),

Frau Maria Jaakkola (Leiterin des Umweltamts und Stadtplanungsamts der Stadt Helsinki),

Herrn Heikki Laaksonen (kommunaler Landschaftsarchitekt der Stadt Kotka) und an Herrn Seppo Närhi (Geschäftsführer der Landscape Contractors Association – Viheralue Rakentajat ry)

Frankreich
Lille, Parc de la Deûle
& Lyon Confluence

Berque, Augustin: Du geste à la cité: Formes urbaines et lien social au Japon. Paris 1993, S. 247

Berque, Augustin: Les raisons du paysage. Paris 1995, S. 192

Blanc, Nathalie: „De l'écologie dans la ville". In: Ethnologie française. Nr. 4/2004, Vol. 34, S. 601–607

Bonnin, Philippe/Clavel, Maïté: „Introduction. Quand la nature s'urbanise". In: Ethnologie française. Nr. 4/2010, Vol. 40, S. 581–587

Bourdin, Alain: „La ville se dit par évaluation". In: Cahiers internationaux de sociologie. Nr. 1/2010, Vol. 128–129, S. 117–134

Décamps, Henri: Ecologie : interfaces et ruptures – Séance solennelle de réception de nouveaux membres de l'Académie des sciences. Geewählt am 16.12.2008 und 24.02.2009

Bernard, Vincent/Deschodt, Laurent/Praud, Ivan et al: Archéoligie en nord – pas-de-Calais. Houplin-Ancoisne „Le marais de Santes" – Parc de la Deûle. Villeneuve-d'Ascq 2004

Dudzinski, Francis: La Deûle : renaissance d'une rivière. Lille 2011, S. 51

Larrère, Catherine: Du bon usage de la nature – Pour une philosophie de l'environnement. Paris 1997, S. 355

Louiset, Odette: „La Ville pour nature". In: L'information géographique. Nr. 3/2010, Vol. 74, S. 6–22

Lyon Confluence: Habiter à la confluence: un quartier actif, mixte et écologique. Lyon 2009, S. 15

Mollie, Caroline: Des arbres dans la ville, l'urbanisme végétal. Arles, Paris 2009, S. 254

Syndicat mixte du Parc de la Deûle: Le parc de la Deûle: des espaces pour découvrir, rêver et mieux vivre. Lille 1997, S. 45

Younès, Chris: Ville contre-nature – Philosophie et architecture. Paris 1999, S. 281

Niederlande
Breda, Borneo & Sporenburg

Adriaanse, Carlinde: On measuring and explaining neighbourhood success : a behavioural economic approach. Amsterdam 2011, S. 184

Aluvihare, Ruwan: A city in progress : physical planning in Amsterdam. Amsterdam 1994

Andela, Gerrie: Im Blickpunkt Niederlande : beispielhafte Ideen und Konzepte für Stadt und Landschaft. München 2002, S. 128

Hoeven, Casper van der/Louwe, Jos: Amsterdam als stedelijk bouwwerk : een morfologische analyse. Amsterdam 2003, S. 165

Hoog, Maurits de: 4x Amsterdam : ontwerpen aan de stad. Bussum 2005, S. 127

Hoog, Maurits de/Vermeulen, Rick: Nieuwe ritmes van de stad : metropoolvorming in Amsterdam. Bussum 2009, S. 111

Koekebakker, Olof: Westergasfabriek culture park : transformation of a former industrial site in Amsterdam. Rotterdam 2003, S. 144

Masboungi, Ariella: Atelier Projet Urbain, Breda, faire la ville durable. Paris 2008, S. 143

Rijs, Jacob van/Winy, Maas: FARMAX : Excursions on Density MVRDV. Rotterdam 2006, S. 736

Reijndorp, Arnold: Stadswijk: stedenbouw en dagelijks leven. Rotterdam 2004, S. 224

Schaap, Ton: Amsterdam. Rotterdam 2008, S. 80

Vereinigtes Königreich
East London & Greenwich Millennium Village

Greater London Authority: East London Green Grid Supplementary Planning Guidance. 2008, S. 65

Department for Communities and Local Government: Thames Gateway Parklands Vision. 2008, S. 37

Meridian Delta limited: Greenwich Millennium Village Design Code. 2004, S. 216

iug
institut d'urbanisme
de grenoble

Verfasser
> Charles Ambrosino,
> Jennifer Buyck,
> Muriel Delabarre,
> Hendrika Kirchhoff,
> Mathieu Perrin,
> Melanie Schulte,
> Marcus Zepf.

Forschungsprojekt
Institut d'Urbanisme de Grenoble
2012–2013

ELCA

EUROPEAN
LANDSCAPE
CONTRACTORS
ASSOCIATION